*This book is dedicated to
our beautiful planet earth.*

Acknowledgment

It would be impossible to write a conventional acknowledgment for this book because no one I know wishes to receive "credit" for the fact that this book has become a reality.

Instead, let me say this. There are many, many people who have contributed their time, money, energy, love, and vision in order that this book would become available to you. Many of these people have demonstrated extraordinary commitment and love so that you, the reader, would also have the opportunity to experience the same freedom, joy, and incredible expansion that they have experienced in the final elimination of the source of fear.

There are people who told me that they "would do anything" to see this book written and published so that this process would be easily available to anyone who wanted it. I want you, the reader, to know this so you will know how precious you are and how important you are, and that, yes, there are people who really do care.

These people are your friends. They are your brothers and sisters in our collective humanity. They did not put out their effort for me or for Telstar. They put their effort out entirely for you. On behalf of them, I wish to convey their love.

Saratoga

The Final Elimination of the Source of Fear

Also by Telstar:

Global Vision: Expanding Business, Trade and Commerce into Global Awareness

The Final Elimination of the Source of Fear

by
Saratoga and Telstar

Nova Publications
P.O. Box 25306
Albuquerque, N.M. 87125

ISBN: 0-9619235-1-2

Library of Congress Catalog Card Number: 96-67059

Published by Nova Publications, P. O. Box 25306, Albuquerque, NM 87125, USA

Printed in the USA by Desert Dreams Publishers
P.O. Box 91825
Albuquerque, NM 87199-1825

About Telstar

Telstar is a power. An infinite energy and force of Nature that is inter-dimensional and Inter-Universal in scope. The name "Telstar" is only a word given for purposes of our understanding on this planet. Beyond the earth, it is not in need of a name, but exists as a pure energy designed to contribute and to facilitate evolution. Our knowledge of this presence that we call Telstar, comes to us in the form of six beings who are named Mikhail, Adam, John, Sangia, Miribi, and Isadora. Saratoga is the spokesperson for these six and also the channel, should the need arise, as they do not live upon our planet, per se, but reside interdimensionally in space.

It would be impossible to describe the experience of knowing these entities. Their beauty is infinite, their love boundless, and their friendship eternal. Their love for this earth is unfailing and they are committed to us completely. They are committed to us experiencing the truth about ourselves and who we are, as love. They are committed to us being completely free from the pain and suffering that has bound us as human beings for so many millenniums. They will do whatever it takes at whatever level we are asking for help, to aid us in eliminating the problem. They are among our dearest friends, and will always remember who we really are, even when we forget and are in our darkest hour. They will hold the light of that truth, no matter what we say in denial of that fact. This book is a gift of love, from them to you, should you desire some additional help in your life.

Contents

Preface

The Final Elimination of the Source of Fear began as a process and an event in the early part of April, 1989. I was living in Santa Fe, New Mexico and had been channeling Telstar regularly for the past two years. One day I noticed that my entire reality was shifting dramatically and I was able to "see" things about our world that I had never seen before. It was as though a veil was lifted and I could clearly distinguish between what was true and a manifestation of love and divine presence, and what was false or artificial and a manifestation of fear and illusion. This experience did not come via mental interpretation. It was different. There was no "thought" involved. It was pure seeing, pure knowing. It was as though someone had opened my eyes and an entire world unfolded before me about what was really going on behind the scenes on this planet. This experience continued for about three days and its intensity grew with every passing hour. I was totally consumed with what I was seeing. By the third day, Mikhail suddenly appeared to me, and with a most amazing demonstration of grace and power, illuminated the entire situation for me in a matter of moments. And then, with a swiftness and sureness that could only be called divine, he eliminated from within me an invisible "something" that would later be called "the source of fear."

I can only tell you that from that moment on, my life was completely changed. When he left, I went out into the yard and sat among the pinions and junipers for several hours. I was stunned, amazed. I could feel the ground beneath me in a whole new way. I wanted to touch everything natural around me. Everything possessed a clarity and a brilliance that was spellbinding! I felt like a child again. I felt the wind on my cheek and the warmth of the sun in ways that gave incredible new dimension to the world around me. I touched the dirt and felt a pine cone. I looked up at the brilliant blue sky and noticed the beautiful contrast of puffy, pure white clouds and the lovely green of tree tops illuminated in the bright afternoon sunlight. Everything was imbued with pure, radiant energy!

My heart filled and all of my senses were alive with the ecstasy of experiencing these beautiful things around me. I heard the wind and smelled the intoxicating desert fragrances. I felt a profound stillness embracing everything with love. It was all so natural! So normal! I realized that there was nothing unusual about any of this. What was unusual was my ability to experience it. Something had left. A barrier was gone, and I felt new energy flowing throughout my being. My emotions were clear. My mind was open and relaxed. My body felt brilliant and alive. Yet it was all so simple! I felt brilliantly charged with the subtleties of infinite energy and Universal life, as were the beautiful things around me. My heart, my mind, and my eyes were clear. An internal "gripped" feeling that had been so familiar was gone! I was free and my senses were awash with something new.

I quietly got up and went back into the house. From that moment on, I was to experience a never-ending power that could serve me from within, to whatever extent I chose to take advantage of the opportunity.

After my experience, I felt imbued with a tremendous power and consciousness for change. I knew, without a doubt, that we, as human beings, are capable of anything and that all things are possible. All that is necessary is to eliminate that certain invisible "something" that keeps us gripped and separated in an experience of pain, doubt, and fear. That keeps us trapped in an experience that we are alone in the Universe and basically unempowered, and must do anything and everything to compensate for that fact in order to survive our time here on planet earth.

I had barely had a moment to contemplate what this experience might mean to others when Telstar produced an event to provide that opportunity entitled "The Final Elimination of the Source of Fear." This event was presented in various, major cities around North America for a period of about six years. During this period of time, Mikhail often expressed a deep desire to see this event manifested in the form of a book, so that the process would be readily available to anyone who desired it without having to attend a live, channeled event, which was expensive and often required travel to a city where it was being held.

So after much hard work, this book has now become a reality. This book was created to be more than just a story to read or to provide information to absorb. It was created with one, single purpose in mind. For you, the reader, to have an opportunity, through the use of this book, to experience the final elimination of the source of fear for yourself.

Saratoga

Chapter 1

What is the Source of Fear?

In order to eliminate a problem it is important, first of all, to admit that there is one. Let us begin by looking at our beautiful planet earth. Is there a problem here? Most people will agree that yes indeed there is a problem, and in fact, there are so many problems that they are far too numerous to count.

But how do we hold the existence of these problems in our minds? Some will say, "Well, there are lots of problems, but there are also many explanations for why they are here." And still others will say, "Well, you know, it's really okay because everything is unfolding according to God's plan." But the most prevalent belief, perhaps, is this one, "Yes, yes, there are many problems here, but you know it's something that we all have to live with, it's a part of life, and there's really nothing we can do about it anyway." End of story.

The overriding assumption is that problems are a part of life and we simply must accept that. Let us define what a problem is. A problem, in simple terms, can be described as an obstacle to the true and full expression of who we really are. In a global sense, our problems are many—war, starvation, poverty, hatred, destruction of our planetary environment, disease, suffering, and an overall climate of unbearable human pain which is currently being shared by all other living creatures on the planet as well. Yet some will continue to say that this is all very necessary on a "spiritual" level, of course. They will tell us that it is a great way for us all to learn and grow and evolve. Then there are those who will say that these terrible problems are necessary in order for us to become "strong" by overcom-

1

ing them. Others will say that these problems are in truth our "punishment" for being the low, unworthy specimens of life (sinners) that we supposedly are.

Let us examine some of these beliefs.

Belief Number 1: The spiritual explanation and "school of learning" theory. If you were a spiritual being, meaning a be-ing of love of course, and someone suggested to you that it would be a good idea to go to a place of tremendous terror, pain, and suffering, and that this would somehow cause you to become even *more* spiritual—meaning to experience more love, of course—what would you say? "Great idea! I'm sure that living in an atmosphere of hatred, pain, and suffering would greatly add to my experience of God. I think I'll go at once. Thanks for the suggestion!" Let's say that you were *not* a spiritual being—meaning that you were somehow "anti-love" for lack of a better word. Would stewing in a climate of more hatred and violence somehow set you straight? Would a nega-tive experience such as that somehow "light your path" and "show you the way" to love and divine truth? Some mistak-enly believe that it will.

Belief Number 2: The "strengthening" theory. This theory sug-gests that as human beings we are inherently weak and if we are given all of these terrible obstacles to overcome, that we will somehow become strong. It implies that if you place an already weak individual in a situation where everything works *against* him or her, that lo and behold that person will feel so uplifted they might overcome all of it and become permanently strong! If this theory is right then perhaps we should assume that we could enhance this wonderful opportunity by placing all sorts of physical obstacles designed to potentially harm us in between our homes and our cars. If we could make it to our cars unhurt, just think of how strong we would feel! Perhaps we could also think of some really mean things to do to our friends in order to provide them with even *more* opportunities to overcome something negative and become strong. If they were to get upset, all we would have to do is happily remind them that our meanness is for their "own good" and that someday they'll thank us for the contribution.

Belief Number 3: The "punishment" theory. This belief is fascinating because it presupposes that a brilliant, all-loving, and intelligent God has created these terrible creatures such as ourselves who can do no right, and this same intelligent, loving God so thoroughly disapproves of his/her mistaken creation of us, that he/she figures the best recourse is to torture us mercilessly with every kind of pain and suffering imaginable. Need we say more?

So what do all of these beliefs have in common? Confusion! Mostly what they have in common is that they are riddled with all sorts of convoluted justifications as to why we are in the collective pain that we have all been suffering for millenniums. How did we come up with these beliefs and why do we continue to have faith in them? The simple truth is that there is *no logical explanation* for why we might deserve the suffering that we endure on this planet. Yet we react to it in much the same way that a child who is abused by a parent might react. The child believes that he/she somehow deserves it, it is the right thing no matter how painful, and that in some bizarre way it is their parent's way of showing love. In other words, it is easier to believe that there is a "good reason" for it, then to simply accept that it's wrong.

So how do we react to the global suffering that we see all around us? The truth is, that in our hearts we can't bear it, yet it is here nonetheless, so we do whatever we can to cope with it. We go into denial. We tell ourselves, "It's not so bad." We

rationalize it. We look away. We find an infinite number of dis-
tractions to avoid it. Drugs, TV, alcohol. All designed to make
us unconscious. We repress our emotions. And for whatever is
left in our conscious experience after all this avoidance, we
justify. This is the reason for all of these beliefs. We feel that we
have to justify the pain in order to live with it.

I once knew a man who was doing some incredibly valuable
work on the planet which showed that he had a tremendous
heart. Yet, he had still rationalized all of the suffering to be
"spiritually important" on "some other level." I challenged him
to go pay a visit to some real, physically starving children, to
sit there with them, look straight into their eyes, and reassure
them that all of their pain was really okay because on some
other level it was spiritually significant. He said he couldn't
do it.

So we make up all of these illusions and hide behind them
in our minds. The truth of the matter is that we cannot in our
heart of hearts accept that this suffering is the truth. We cannot, in any true experience of love, believe that we *should*, for
whatever reason, endure so much pain and struggle. So why
does it exist?

The Source of Fear

In order to understand that there *is* a problem and then to
ultimately identify it, we must first examine our notions about
what it means to be a human being and what it means to be
alive.

The one, most significant assumption that has kept us
trapped in our pain and struggle for so many eons is the assumption that love and hate are both equal and valid emotions and that they *naturally* coexist within our human experi-

4

ence. We believe that God has created us this way on purpose. We feel that we are in some kind of a "test." We believe that it is our job on earth to overcome the hate and live from love. We believe that God sanctions this inner battle and that it is our job to somehow pass the test and win on the side of love. Has anyone ever asked themselves why an intelligent God would have a need for such bizarre recreation as putting us through this horrific test, with no instructions, and watching us struggle to succeed through so much pain?

In accepting this duality and this pain as a part of life, we have thus defined a human being as a struggling individual who is inherently flawed by nature of design. Have you heard the phrase, "I'm only human?" What does this mean? It is an indication that we view ourselves as weak, unworthy entities who can't really be expected to succeed.

The reason that this assumption is deadly is because if we choose to identify ourselves with the problem and say it is a part of *who we are,* as human beings, then we have no chance and no hope of ever eliminating it. How can we eliminate something that is us? We can't! And if we can't, then we are hopelessly doomed to live with it forever and possibly destroy ourselves in the process. Yet that level of hopelessness can't be reconciled either, can it? It is therefore imperative that we redefine ourselves as human beings from what we know to be the truth in our hearts.

Have you ever done something that was really strange, something that you would interpret as negative, and thought to yourself, "I don't know why I'm doing this. This is not how I really feel at all." Have you ever looked at what you might interpret as your personality "flaws" and been confused and frustrated as to why they are there, because they don't really feel like the real *you*? The chances are that you have had many

5

hints throughout your life in the form of recognizing, on a very deep level, your own divine brilliance. How many people are walking around secretly knowing that they are capable of *incredible* things, and in their hearts they have a tremendous desire for that manifestation, and yet are totally confused as to why they also feel that they *can't*.

If we are true to what we know in our deepest hearts, we know that we are essentially beings of love. We are brilliant, creative beings of great strength and purpose. We are also caring, sensitive, and extraordinarily appreciative of the great beauty of life. We love harmony. We seek peace. We love to love. We are Gods. We are here to contribute. We have great purpose. In short, a human being is meant to be an extension and an expression of Omnipresent Love. There is no "test." It is already who we are. If we can accept that this is the only real *truth* about what it means to be a human being, then the next question becomes obvious. How is it, if we are love, that we manage to perform so many abominable acts on our beautiful earth? What is all of this weakness really about? If we are capable of performing acts of hatred when the only *truth* is that we are love, then that clearly indicates that there is some additional principle "hiding" in our consciousness which makes those negative acts possible.

This principle is what we will call the "source of fear." This book will explain, in detail, what that principle is and how it works. For now, however, we will offer you a general description of what it is and what it feels like to live with it.

The source of fear is an invisible, energetic phenomenon. It is impossible to locate it on a "physical" level, yet the symptoms of its existence are everywhere. The greatest reason for our failure on this planet to overcome our most serious problems of hatred, violence, and pain, is that we have only dealt with the symptoms of the problem and never with the source. Even worse, we have identified *ourselves* as being the source of the problem, which is why there has been so much killing of one another for centuries.

Interestingly enough, no matter how many people you kill, the problem doesn't go away, does it? In fact, it only gets worse.

Now some people might say, "I really don't have time for all of these global problems. I am completely overcome with problems of my own and my hands are full with my *own* life."

Here we can make an important point about dealing with this energetic phenomenon that we are calling the source of fear. You most likely have picked up this book from a desire to deal with this problem inside of yourself. Perhaps you have interpreted it as a personal problem that can be effectively approached by simply dealing with your personal situation. The source of fear is, in reality, an *evolutionary* problem of massive proportions. It has been with us for thousands of years. It is something that is experienced by all of us on a collective level, and felt intensely and individually on a personal level. In order to deal with any problem effectively, you must address it in the proper context. The only context within which we can effectively address the source of fear is the context of our collective, human evolution. From that greater context, an understanding can be gained about precisely what it means to you, the individual, in your personal life.

Let us therefore discuss the source of fear on an individual level. As much as is possible, we would like to suggest that you look for your own experience of everything that we are talking about rather than blindly believing everything that we say. That way, we can parallel each other in strength and address this issue from a co-creative place, which will add a great deal more power to the process for you.

What does the source of fear feel like and how can we identify it experientially? The experience of the principle itself is subtle, because it is so much in the background of all of the symptoms. The symptoms themselves are easy to identify. They manifest in a wide range of negative experiences such as hatred, violence, anger, fear, destructiveness (self and other), boredom, procrastination, ill health, loneliness, feeling trapped, guilt, insecurity, conflict, unworthiness, need, greed, anxiety, control, repetitive behavior patterns, prejudice, addictions, dysfunctional relationships, repression, confusion, indecisiveness, worry, emotional withdrawal, the list goes on and on . . . . This ongoing list of negatives is simply clear and undeniable evidence that the source of fear exists. Remember, if there was not some underlying principle behind all of these things, then none of these experiences would be possible. It is the principle itself that causes us to be able to have these experiences at all.

So what does it feel like to experience the principle itself? An experience of the source of fear can be best described as a feeling of being energetically "gripped" in any of the aforementioned negative experiences. It is the feeling of being seized by an inner experience of fear, anger, or repression that makes one feel powerless, in that moment, to change. The source of fear is the reason that a person can devote years to psychoanalysis, personal growth, or some other method of individual change and still be met with the endless frustration of recurring patterns that simply will not go away.

This *sensation* of being uncontrollably *gripped* or *seized* by a negative inner experience is the simplest way to describe an experience of the source of fear. The source of fear cannot be "overcome." The only viable action is for it to be permanently eliminated. Otherwise you have no alternative but to live with it and try to overcome the negative patterns of emotion, thought, and behavior that it leaves in its wake. What happens to these patterns if you eliminate the source of fear? You will then find yourself on a very different course. You will no longer be forced to live with these problems if you don't want to, with your only option being to try and *overcome* them as though you were trying to climb over some permanent kind of obstacle that is in the way of your expression. Instead, you will find yourself able to live in the true power of who you are, with the ability to *move through* these problems in such a way as to *transmute* them permanently. We are talking about the difference between having to live with these problems and overcome them in order to become strong, and *starting off strong*, exercising your innate strength to go forward and move through these obstacles in such a way that they permanently disappear. The more that you do this and transmute these patterns of fear, anger, and negativity, the more your light will shine and the more of *you* there will be to express itself in the truth of love, light, exuberance, health, happiness, and profound creativity. What is important to understand is that the source of fear is what *holds* all of the patterns together and keeps them intact, and causes more and more of them to occur. It can make it almost impossible to get rid of unwanted things about yourself. It can severely impede, if not totally stop your evolutionary flow of expansion. To eliminate the problem, to permanently eliminate its *source*, is the only possible solution. The miracle of this time is that we are finally in a place to do it.

Many people have wondered for centuries, where is the help and when will it come? We have blamed the Universe, we have blamed God, we have blamed anything and everything we could think of. Did you know that at our first cries for help, those cries were answered? We were immediately met, although we did not realize it, with powerful forces of nature and evolution designed to evolve us, no matter how long it took, to a place of strength and clarity where we could finally look at this phenomenon, called the source of fear, and see it for ourselves. And more importantly, to evolve us to a place where *finally* we would possess the necessary strength and clarity to enable us to cease our tolerance of this phenomenon once and for all. Why did it take so long? Because the only way to eliminate it is through an act of our own will and consciousness. We had to evolve to a level of love for ourselves coupled with a love of life and truth, where we would be willing to hold a standard of that truth in our hearts and minds, above all else. This would enable us to clearly and sincerely intend the final elimination of the source of fear. We had to believe that we are love. Thus we would finally be in a position to align ourselves with the forces of light, truth and love, the very forces that create the Universe itself, and finally experience the relief that we have for so long deeply sought within ourselves.

For all of this time, we have thought that we were waiting for the Universe, waiting for a "savior." The truth, dear friends, is that everything has, in actuality, been waiting for us. The time has come. We have finally arrived.

Chapter 2

Getting Ready

The purpose of this chapter is to assist you in getting ready to experience the process which will ultimately lead to the final elimination of the source of fear. The great thing about this process is that it's very simple. All you have to do is read the book! But it is important to prepare a context for your reading so that it will lead to the desired result.

A great deal of work has gone into the creation of this book so that it can provide you with much more than just a reading experience. How you approach it will make all the difference. In writing this book we endeavored to put our live event entitled "The Final Elimination of the Source of Fear" into a written form that could align you with the powerful forces of Nature and Evolution that are specifically designed to help you eliminate the source of fear. The source of fear cannot be eliminated simply by thinking about it in your mind, nor by reading about it in a book. It requires a synergistic act of Nature, God, and evolution which includes *you* and your will or desire to experience this result. The purpose of the book is simply to align your consciousness and help you become as clear as possible about exactly what it is we are talking about eliminating. The more clear you become about what the source of fear is and how deeply it affects your life and the lives of everyone on the planet, the more natural your desire to want to have it eliminated. Which brings us to the point of how to approach this book. We suggest that you begin by looking into your heart and asking yourself if you deeply desire to have the source of fear eliminated from within yourself. This process is designed to work *with* you in conjunction with your own desire. If you approach it from a skeptical place or a frightened place, those thoughts and emotions will block your ability to participate in the process with your own consciousness. Instead you will find yourself standing back and "observing," which means that one very essential ingredient will be missing from the process. That essential ingredient is *you*. If *you* are not there, the process cannot work for you.

If you do not have a real desire to have the source of fear eliminated from within you, but are intrigued nonetheless, then by all means feel free to just read the book for information's sake and have an enjoyable time doing it. It is quite possible that later on you might experience the desire to have this experience for yourself, in which case you can always come back to it and approach it as a process.

If, on the other hand, you are a person who has been looking for an answer for yourself and are deeply longing for that answer to appear, then perhaps this is the moment you've been waiting for. There are people who will simply read the title of this book and immediately experience a recognition of something that they have been looking for. They may not be able to explain it, but they will know through some deep inner sense that this is what they have been seeking.

Other people will be in a place of having tried *everything* they know in an attempt to free themselves from some invisible "something" that makes them feel trapped from within. Perhaps some of the words spoken so far will spark a connection that this is the answer to a prayer. And you might be a person who is somewhere in the middle. But the most important thing in the beginning, if you want to experience success, is to simply be able to say to yourself (in your own way, of course), "Yes, I do want to have the source of fear permanently eliminated from within me."

The process, as it is laid down in this book, simply consists of reading the entire book from cover to cover. It does not require any additional work on your part. At some point, toward the end of the book, you will be invited to follow some very simple instructions, almost like a meditation procedure, during which time you will have the opportunity to experience the final elimination of the source of fear for yourself.

The results are permanent. Once the source of fear is eliminated, you cannot get it back. Why? Because evolution only goes forward. And the final elimination of the source of fear is an evolutionary act. There would be absolutely no point in nature creating a process entitled the final elimination of the source of fear, if you could somehow go back to where you were, have it come back again, and have to start all over.

The Process

During the course of reading the book, you might experience various emotions, depending upon how involved you have allowed yourself to be with the information.

Remember that you cannot eliminate the source of fear all by yourself. For those of you who might take offense at this fact, look closely for a moment at how nature works. Nothing in nature exists in a void. We, as humans upon this earth, sometimes like to fancy ourselves as these rugged individualists whose ultimate goal is to be able to do everything by ourselves. We have taken this belief to such an extreme that we even believe that we can destroy nature for commercial purposes and that somehow that won't affect us. I suppose we can create some illusion about "standing on our own" by blocking certain things out of our consciousness. But let's look at the truth. We cannot exist without food, water, and air to breathe. We certainly require our planet to live on. Our planet requires the sun. We need all of the elements of the earth in order to live and have substance from which to create. Even the cells in our bodies are dependent upon one another. And these are just physical requirements. What about other requirements that we cannot see? How about that which produces life itself? What about the ultimate force of life that grows every living thing and evolves each of us into greater and greater manifestations of ourselves? And everything that exists completely rests upon powerful Universal principles and laws of creation that are not within our domain to control.

Our earth is but a tiny speck in a vast realm of Universal creation and thought. If you can surrender to that fact and realize that the final elimination of the source of fear requires a vast, synergistic interplay of many wonderful, powerful forces of nature, then you will have an easier time just flowing with yourself and your emotions throughout the course of this book. Otherwise you might be tempted to try to take "control" of the source of fear, and attempt to dominate it, which will only make things worse. This is something a person would do only if they had to do it alone. There is a much better way! That is the way of surrender and faith. Surrender to the love that you feel in your heart and faith in the power of that love. The whole Universe responds to a sincere being. It is not necessary to know everything all by yourself. So with that in mind, let's describe some of the emotions that you might encounter during your journey, while you contemplate the contents of this book.

The source of fear itself is based upon a simple principle known as resistance. This resistance factor can create a wall to Universal support, which can actually cause you to perceive help as a threat. The reason for this is that the existence of the source of fear is based solely upon survival. It survives by remaining hidden and unconscious. The more that we expose the source of fear, the more empowered we become in our consciousness to eliminate it. Yet at the same time, you might also experience feelings of profound resistance. The resistance is there because the more exposure, the greater the threat. This resistance can take many forms. We have found, during the course of presenting our live events, that discussing this resistance prior to engaging the process, can substantially lessen the chances of it coming up, because it is exposed prior to it taking hold. One very predictable way that this resistance could manifest is in the form of negative thoughts designed to turn you against the material in this book. (Remember the help being perceived as a threat?) Although this book is dealing with some very intense subject matter (namely, the main problem that we have been experiencing on our planet for thousands of years) it is still meant to be a very friendly process and a tremendously loving process as well. There is meant to be a sense of freedom and good will surrounding our entire interaction. It is one thing not to agree with what you are reading (that's fine-it's what is known as freedom of choice), but if you are feeling intensely *threatened* by what is being said, then you may want to consider that what you are experiencing is resistance being generated by the source of fear itself. For what better way to sabotage your chances for experiencing the final elimination of the source of fear than to cause you to perceive the help designed to bring you there as an enemy and a threat?

Some of the other forms that this resistance might take are procrastination (an unwillingness to finish the book or putting it off), and laziness (saying it doesn't matter and it's not important, anyway). This is particularly true if you started off feeling very "gung-ho" and excited about doing it. Another form of resistance might take the form of putting it off until things are "just perfect" or "absolutely right" and then realizing after a point that it never seems to be that way.

In reading the book, you might experience a profound level of unconsciousness or "sleepiness." You might find yourself reading whole pages, or even chapters, and feeling as though nothing registers. This is because in recognizing the information that you are reading, you will penetrate very deep levels of unconsciousness surrounding the source of fear. Sometimes people are affected by this and actually *experience* the unconsciousness, and other times they do not. Whether you do or not, does not in any way prohibit a positive outcome.

How to Read the Book

It is not necessary to *remember* everything that you read in order to experience a successful result. In fact, if you try too hard to retain the information, in such a way as to process and store it for later use, you might actually interfere with the process itself. The best approach is to read the book naturally, do your best to comprehend what you are reading, *as you read it*, and then let go of it as you go on to the next page. The book will lead you through this process in its own way. It is not necessary to try and *force* your mind to interpret it and make it fit in with what you already know. The best thing to do is to *relax* and have faith in your ability to comprehend naturally, as you read. The important thing is to surrender to the process and not worry about storing information. Remember, the reading itself will create the process. All you have to do is read. It's designed to be simple! Another way to make the process easier is to avoid the temptation of thinking about how you might *use* this information and apply it in your life. If you're trying to figure it out and draw conclusions prematurely, you will create a very unnecessary struggle for yourself. Try to remember that you only need to do this process *once*. The process is self-contained. The results are permanent. From there, you can go out and experience the tremendous freedom of knowing that you have the power to change, however you want to, and create your life as you see fit.

Other Emotions and Thoughts

As in any deep process, be prepared for the possibility that certain emotions might surface as a result of the work you are doing within your consciousness.

Over the years, as we have presented our live event, we have noticed that there are certain emotions, thoughts, and feelings that tend to come up for people just in the course of the process itself. These experiences will tend to intensify as a person is getting closer to the moment when they will have a chance to experience the final elimination of the source of fear. In a moment, we will give you a list of potential thoughts and feelings that you might encounter as you read the book, if you are using the book as a process and intend to experience the elimination of the source of fear for yourself. It is also possible, on the other hand, that you will not experience any of these thoughts and feelings and instead will feel tremendous elation and excitement as you sail through the entire process effortlessly! And then again, you might end up feeling quite neutral, take the whole thing in stride, and still experience a miraculous result. In short, it doesn't really matter what you experience, in terms of your success. There is such a wide range of ways in which people go through this process within themselves, that it is best not to judge any one way as being better or worse than another. The best thing to do is to simply accept however it is for you and continue on with your experience. No two people will ever be exactly alike in this situation. But in the event that it might help you to recognize certain things in advance, here is a list of some very common thoughts and feelings that people often have during their process:

1) Severe doubt that it will ever work for you. This feeling is almost universal and manifests as a tremendous fear of "I think that this will work for everyone but me. I'll be the one exception!" This thought tends to intensify more and more as you get closer to the actual experience of eliminating the source of fear.

2) A barrage of negative thoughts and feelings where your mind thinks intense thoughts *against* you, and reminds you of all the other times in your life where you were excited about succeeding at something and then failed. It brings up every broken hope and dream in living, 3D color, and tries to convince you that this situation will only bring you more of the same disappointment.

3) Boredom, frustration, and impatience. This can manifest as a feeling of, "Enough already! I'm tired of talking about this. Do we have to go on and on? I just want to get this over with." This is a manifestation of attempted sabotage resulting from the source of fear itself. It is an attempt to convince you to do the final process prematurely, before your consciousness is fully prepared for it, in which case you cannot experience a successful result. It is always justified by saying that you've "heard enough" and already know that you want it eliminated, so why wait?

4) Confusion. This thought manifests itself as, "I can't figure out where all of this is going. Something must be wrong. I don't understand what's going on." This is actually a sign, from the influence of the source of fear, that there is a fear of losing control.

5) Unexplained anxiety and/or fear. This generally means

18

that the source of fear is being catalyzed and is imminently close to being successfully eliminated. This "catalyzing" can still happen, however, without you feeling any fear or anxiety at all!

6) Unusual physical symptoms. Sometimes the physical body will react in peculiar ways to the changes occurring within. People have reported headaches, indigestion, and various aches and pains, particularly if the source of fear has had an unusually strong affect on their physical body. These symptoms almost always disappear completely the moment that the source of fear is eliminated.

Again, remember that you might experience some of these, all of these, or *none* of these and still have a successful outcome. The important thing is not to judge yourself. None of the above experiences can ultimately interfere with a successful end result. If your heart is sincere and you really do want to experience the final elimination of the source of fear, then all you have to do is simply stay with the process and keep reading. It's that simple!

Additional Ways to Ensure Your Success

By now you might have figured out that the only way to interfere with your chances of successfully experiencing the final elimination of the source of fear is to abandon the process before it is complete, stop reading the book, or take short cuts and jump to the final process prematurely.

You might say, "Well, that sounds easy. All I have to do is stay with the book until I've finished reading it." And you'd be right. It *is* that easy, if your heart is sincere and you remain open.

The most important thing to consider, however, is the resistance that might come up inside of you because of the obvious threat that this process poses to the source of fear itself. Therefore, we would like to give you a few simple tips to help yourself, if this resistance becomes a problem for you and you still want to experience the final elimination of the source of fear.

Point 1. This first point pertains to making a group effort or finding a partner. If you are having trouble staying with the book on your own, you might get together with a friend or family member who also wants to go through the process. It is also possible that you might want to work together with a small group of friends in a similar way as you might to form a study group. If you choose to work together with someone else, you should make sure of several things.

    a. Each person sincerely, in their own heart, should want to experience the results of the process. You cannot talk anyone into this or try to convince them. If you do, you will only end up with an unwilling participant who is forcing themselves to do something that they don't really feel to do for themselves. The process will not work for them and their unnatural participation will only slow things down for you. People should feel naturally inspired to do this process and the feeling should come from them.

    b. Avoid working with skeptical people who have a "prove-it-to-me" attitude. These people are hoping to prove that it doesn't work and will have all of their energy invested in achieving *no* result. Happily, for them, they will achieve just that, but you will be left feeling totally unsupported and drained of energy.

    c. Keep it simple. Don't try to create elaborate rules for your participation together and most of all, *do not* try to interpret each others process! The process itself is extremely personal and totally unique for each individual. Allow each of you to have your own experience. Remember, you are together simply to provide mutual support to complete the process, not to interpret how each other is doing.

d. Never compare yourself to someone else. There is no way to measure who is doing "better" or "worse." The only thing you can be sure of is that each person will probably respond differently.

e. Most importantly, if you choose to work with someone else and you find that you are not happy with the arrangement, and that it is not working out for you in a favorable way, then *by all means* politely tell the other person or persons that you've decided that you would rather do the process alone or in some other setting. You do not need to feel apologetic about this. Everyone must find their own path, one that they feel the most comfortable in. Remember, it's the *results* that count, not who you do the process with. No one's process is dependent on another person being there.

The best way to approach this process with another person or a small group of people is to remember that you must each function independently in terms of your experience. You must find your own balance together which will allow you to do this. It might be as simple as just sharing your experience with each other, without judgment. It should never be done in a situation that involves struggle or conflict. If this happens, and it cannot be resolved quickly and easily, then everyone should graciously let go and allow each person to pursue their own path individually.

Point 2. Do not put pressure on yourself to "succeed" as you are not able to do this alone. The Universe is completely available to help you with this, as are the powerful forces of Nature and evolution. The energy and divine presence that is there to help you already knows that you might feel doubtful, unsure, or afraid. All of those emotions (plus many others) have already been taken into account so as not to impair your result.

Point 3. Before you begin the process, you might have trouble believing in it and could have thoughts such as , "This can't be possible. It sounds too good to be true. It sounds too simple." What you must realize is that we have collectively been evolving toward this moment for many hundreds or even thousands of years. Individually, your whole life has been preparing you for this moment. The truth is that most of the work has already been done before you even picked up this book.

Point 4. Remember that this is a process that you will only need to do *once*, once you are successful. You do not have to go out in your life and "work on" the source of fear. The truth is that there is no way to work on it and make it better. It is what it is, by nature of design and cannot be made into a positive thing. The only possible solution is to permanently eliminate it.

Ultimately, you must do this process in an atmosphere and a setting in which you feel most comfortable. Try to relax as best you can, have faith in God, life, and the power of the Universe to support Love, Light, and Truth. If you don't believe in God, then it's all right. Just simply have faith in your heart. Love is the ultimate, no matter by what name it is called.

Are you ready to begin? Great! Please have a most wonderful experience!

Chapter 3

Radiating Flow & Reverse Flow

There is a power of love that is so great, that exists within us as human beings, that seeks only to express itself outwardly in a profound manifestation of itself. This energy of love is what we will term our divine, human presence. It is the only truth about who we are and this divine presence sources itself in the Universe and beyond. Ultimately, it sources itself in what we will call Omnipresence, the profound oneness that exists behind all things.

You might say that in truth we are an extension of love itself. We are created as Love in human form. Now many people will, of course, dispute this and say, "Oh, really? Then what about all of this killing, and hurting, and pain that is constantly being inflicted by human hands?" We are about to begin a journey which will lead us to the exact and specific answer to that question.

In order to begin this journey, however, we must start with a note of truth. We must create for ourselves a platform of understanding that is based only in truth, and truth alone. Otherwise, how are we to find the real answer to this question?

So with that agreement, let us once again acknowledge that truth, which is that we, as human beings, are love. Period. There is no "and also this" or "and also that." We are love. From that premise, dear friends, it is possible to understand everything.

Let us now examine the very nature of love and how that energy flows in a manifestation of itself. Love is so profound and so utterly powerful that it cannot be contained in any sort of a finite space. Therefore, it is infinite in its existence. In its infinite nature, which is so profound that it cannot even be spoken about, it is so filled with power that it literally becomes light. It is a light that is so awesome that it is beyond comprehension. This light is so powerful that it literally radiates into creation. It pervades everything. It is beyond life, as we understand it, for it creates everything, even life itself.

Love moves forward and seeks always to express itself. This it does through what we will call a radiating flow of energy. Think about your own body for a moment. Is it not a vehicle that is designed solely for the purpose of your own self-expression? To understand this fully, it is important to recognize that the "you" who is meant to do the expressing is love. If you are love, which you are, then that means that your self-expression in its truest form will always follow a path of radiating flow, or put another way, the path of love. In other words, you are meant to exist as an expression of love. This means, then, that your human body is specifically designed to conduct the energetic flow of that love. It is the flow of love, existing as a radiating flow of energy, that moves outward from its central source, or heart, which is the only thing that will ever feel comfortable, natural, or real to your physical human body.

Let us perform a simple experiment, in our minds eye, to illustrate how this works. Imagine yourself seated in a lovely room filled with 100 other people. Picture everyone sitting comfortably together in such a way that everyone can easily join hands. Now as everyone joins hands, you all close your eyes and take a very deep, relaxing breath. Ahhh... As you sit there together, you each perform the very same exercise that you will now perform yourself, in your imagination. Take another deep breath. Ahhh... Relax and allow your physical body to let go. Now take a moment and quietly extend your heart-felt love to every other person in the room, that they might become happy and receive whatever it is that they need in life to be totally fulfilled as human beings. Offer them your heartfelt love and support that they will experience all that they desire in life and be supremely happy and fulfilled.

Take another deep breath. Ahhh... Now contemplate the people outside of this room and extend your love and support toward everyone on the planet. Offer everyone on earth your heartfelt love and support that each person alive today might become truly happy and fulfilled.

Now contemplate the realm of nature, beginning with the kingdom of animals, birds, fishes, and all of the living creatures that live on the earth. Extend your heartfelt love and support that every one of these bright-eyed, living creatures will exist in peace and harmony and have all that they need to live fully and completely on this beautiful planet.

Now contemplate the massive kingdom of trees, plants, and flowers. Offer these wondrous entities your unconditional love and support that they might flourish and grow and be nurtured by the earth itself.

And, finally, contemplate the elements of the earth itself. The huge bodies of water, the land, the clouds, the sky, the vast ranges of mountains, the rock, and the soil. Offer your love and unconditional support and appreciation for this vast and powerful kingdom.

And now embrace the earth with love. Feel your heartfelt love for this planet, your home. And now extend your love beyond the planet itself, into space, and embrace the entire solar system of planets that revolve around our sun. Our neighbors in space. Embrace the sun. Feel the love in your heart for this glorious being and all that it provides. And now extend your love into the galaxy. Embrace the stars, the planets, the moons, the countless interstellar phenomena that make up our galactic home in space. And finally, extend your love out into the Universe, that you might embrace all of space, all life, and include that love within your heart.

Now, be at peace within yourself, and slowly bring your consciousness back into the room that you have shared with the other 100 people. Imagine again that you have all been performing this exercise together. Take another deep breath. All together. Ahhhh... Now, very slowly, begin to open your eyes....

Can you feel how wonderful it feels to exist in a radiating flow? Did you notice that no one had to be taught how to do this? The mere suggestion alone was enough.

Now see if you can breathe quietly for a moment and notice how your body feels as you contemplate this experiment. Does it feel wonderful? Natural? Effortless?

This is the path of love, to move outward in a radiating flow. Now here is something else very interesting to note. If we go back into the room where you were seated with 100 other people, you will remember that everyone was doing this exercise at the same time. Do you remember when each of you was offering your heartfelt love and support to everyone else in the room? Everyone was doing that for everyone else. This means that every single person in the room was receiving the unconditional love and support of every other person there. Imagine yourself in that place once again. You are now receiving the unconditional love and support of everyone else in the room. And so is every other person! All at the same time. Here is an interesting question to ask. Did you or anyone else have to expend any energy trying to *get* this love from anyone else there? No. Amazingly enough, all anyone had to do was something that comes so naturally which is to extend a heartfelt feeling of love and support toward everyone else present.

Rather like the sun. All that the sun has to do is just be what it is and in its natural presence of self, it emanates its light and radiates its own power and brilliance naturally. This bright, radiant light extends everywhere in space and bathes all of life around it with its radiant glow and energy. Such is the nature of a radiating flow. It reaches everyone, all at once. Does anyone have to try and *get* sunlight, when in the presence of the sun? Of course not. It is already a given. You simply relax and receive what is already there.

Love moves outward from a human being in the same way that light emanates outward from the sun. That is why it is so easy to love everyone, all at once. It is also why it is so difficult to love only some people, but not others. Can you imagine what it would be like for the sun to shine only on "certain" people? How might this be accomplished? Well, it would have to block out huge portions of itself and be very controlled as to when and where it could shine.

Now let's imagine what it would be like if everyone on the planet were performing this little experiment all at the same time. Imagine how it might feel if every one of our 5½ billion human relatives were to spend a few moments together and silently extend their heartfelt love and support to everyone else on the face of the earth. This would then mean that each and every human being alive today would be simultaneously receiving the unconditional love and support of everyone else living on the planet. Can you imagine how it would feel to receive the unconditional love and support of your entire human family, all 5½ billion people, all at the same time? All there just for you? And amazingly enough, each and every person would be having the same experience. What if we began to live this way from this moment on? The entire environment within which we all live would *completely* change.

27

Now let us conduct our first experiment with 100 people in a different way. Let's go back into the room where everyone is seated. This time we are going to do something slightly different. Only this time, don't imagine yourself in this picture. Let's just see, hypothetically, what might happen if we were to do the following. Let us say that the idea in this second experiment is for every person in the room to try and *solicit* the unconditional love and support of everyone else in the room. In order to do this, we would have to allow each person an opportunity to stand up in front of everyone else and present to them all of the reasons *why* that person believes that he or she should be loved and supported by the entire group. We would probably have to put a time limit on this and allow each individual a maximum of 15 minutes apiece within which to do this. In that 15 minutes of time, each person would have to *convince* the rest of the people that he or she is *worth* supporting and *worth* loving. Can you imagine the climate in this scenario? First of all, everyone would be extremely nervous as each person experienced extreme anxiety over whether they would succeed or fail at soliciting this love and support from everyone else. People would only be half listening to the speaker as each person became more and more anxious and preoccupied with what they might say when it was their turn to speak. Eventually the whole environment would degenerate into one of guilt, fear, and even lying as people began to just "say" that they loved every person standing up, whether they felt it or not. The entire atmosphere would become totally artificial as this would be the only way to cope with the fear, pain, and unpleasantness of it all. In other words, everyone would start to rationalize that it would be better to just *say* that you loved someone, regardless of how you really felt, because it would be much better for everyone than the honesty of saying that you didn't feel anything, you were afraid, or that what you *really* wanted to do was just get the heck out of there!

And this little scenario would take a total of 24 hours to complete, with no breaks and no rest because those things would make it take even longer. What if each person found themselves trapped in this situation and unable to leave until everyone had been successful at getting the love and support of everyone else? Wouldn't things start to become very political? Deals would be happening everywhere. "You love me for this and I'll love you for that." Eventually a system of management would have to be adopted throughout the room to make sure that everyone was telling the truth and to also discover some way of *measuring* how well everyone was doing in order to prove the result. The resulting problems and complications would be overwhelming.

Now imagine this scenario happening worldwide, on a global level, with all 5½ billion people trying to get the love and unconditional support of everyone else. What would that look like? Well, it would look exactly like what is happening in the world today!

This entire second experiment is an example of what we will call a *reverse-flow* of energy. What this means is that each person's energy is moving inward, or back toward themselves, in exact opposition to who they really are, as each one attempts to solicit the love and support of every other person. In other words, each person's primary motive is to *get* something from everyone else. There is no consciousness of other people because all of the consciousness is on each person's own self. The energetic void that this creates in the surrounding environment is tremendously painful, and unfortunately, only causes more fear and anxiety in the resulting lack, which then causes everyone to do even *more* of the same. The experience of this resulting void convinces everyone that there really *isn't* enough, and that they must try even harder to get what they need for themselves, in order to survive.

A reverse-flow of energy can be compared to suction, or a movement of energy designed to *take* something from the surrounding environment. It is most definitely the energy of fear. What we will find out, as we continue our process, is exactly how this reverse-flow of energy occurs and what is its source.

But for right now, let's examine the basic nature of a radiating flow of energy and then what happens in reverse-flow, so that you can clearly see the difference.

A radiating flow of energy is natural to who we are. Our bodies, minds, and emotions are made to conduct this flow. You can easily see that it is our basic nature to live in a radiating flow, because it is a wonderful experience and it feels good. When we exist in a radiating flow of energy we experience joy, happiness, fulfillment, empowerment, and an unlimited potential for creative expansion. A radiating flow of energy therefore becomes the premise of truth upon which all of our knowledge can be based.

A reverse-flow of energy simply means that something has gone awry in our system. It is termed "reverse" because it exists in exact opposition to the truth of our radiating flow of presence and who we truly are. It is important here to remember that the only truth is that of a radiating flow! We can't change that truth, we can't stop it, we can't make it go away. It is the premise upon which the entire Universe is based.

A reverse-flow would simply mean that the truth is not being experienced. A reverse-flow of energy indicates that something is "missing" in that person's experience. The resulting lack produces experiences of need, fear, and greed whereby a person expends all of their energy in reverse of what is natural. While love is easy to understand and recognize, reverse-flow is far more complicated and insidious. It masquerades easily as something that it is *not*. For example, a person might say that they "love" someone when in truth what they really feel is need and desperation. The more desperate the need, the greater, they will tell you, is the "love." They have taken the need, which is the exact reversal of love, and termed it to be love because they are unable to tell the difference. To that person, love is love, whether it is radiating outward or flowing in reverse. What they don't understand, however, is that love flowing "backwards" isn't love at all. It is a manifestation of emptiness, need, and ultimately fear. It is, in truth, a demonstration that the experience of love is missing. If a person does not feel love within themselves, and therefore needs it from someone else, can they love that other person? Or can they only try to *get* that person's love to replace the missing experience within themselves? Remember this. A radiating flow always *contributes* something into life. A reverse-flow, on the other hand, *takes* energy from the surrounding environment. Remember also that taking is not the same as receiving. Do not confuse reverse-flow with the natural outgoing and ingoing rhythms of giving and receiving. If you observe your breath, you will see what we mean by this. In breathing normally, your body experiences a wonderful ease and an effortless rhythm as air moves in and out of the body via the powerful magnetic energy of life. These in and out movements are so united with one another, that they can actually be experienced as one beautiful cycle of giving and receiving energy in a way that is connected to the whole Universe and ultimately produces life.

Now let's say that something interfered with your breath and temporarily prevented you from breathing. You would suddenly experience a tremendous need for air, right? There would be only one thing on your mind and in the mind of every other cell in your body. To *get* some air! Now! The moment that you could, you would experience gasping and the sucking of air into your lungs to fulfill your need. In that moment, you would not be experiencing the natural cycle of rhythmic breathing. Your body would be poised only for *taking* the air necessary for your survival.

Reverse-flow is like having an interrupted experience of love that never goes away. Unfortunately, the need can never be fulfilled until the love is restored. A person existing in reverse-flow will endlessly seek fulfillment of his or her need, only to find that their environment of life is so depleted from this "taking" flow of energy, that their needs are never met and the harder they try, the more they need.

Reverse flow can easily be recognized by certain characteristics. There is always an element of need or taking. Some examples might be: a very insecure person, who needs recognition from others; a very angry person, who needs others to do battle with; extreme poverty, which is the absence of wealth and produces a tremendous need for money and resources; or, severe illness, which indicates the absence of health and sets up a tremendous physical need in the body. There is also an element of resistance or withholding in reverse-flow. Some examples of this might be: a very shy person who resists and withholds their own self-expression, a very lonely person who resists intimacy with others, a person who gets lost in the crowd as being very ordinary because they resist expressing their own beauty, uniqueness, and creativity, and a person who is perpetually bored because they resist their natural inclination to be involved with life.

In every case there is little or no energy flowing outward

from these people. It appears that their energy is in a state of "arrest" on some level. They have a draining effect on the world around them, and have little or no way to contribute anything. Their lives have little purpose or meaning except towards their own survival. In short, their experience of participation with life has been abducted somehow. Can you imagine a world filled with people like this? Imagine no further, for we are living in one right now.

In extreme cases, reverse flow manifests in a destructive way. When the fear is so great, the level of resistance becomes profound and people will actually begin to destroy things and each other as a manifestation of their pain. All that you have to do is look at the systematic destruction of our earth and its natural environment to see that this is so. The withholding of energy is also profound when you recognize that on a planet of great abundance, with unlimited potential for its natural, human inhabitants, that almost everyone is starving. They are starving for food, starving for shelter, starving for opportunity, starving for love, starving for just about everything that is natural to who we are.

What is causing this withholding of energy and how can it be corrected? Let's find out.

Chapter 4

Omnipresence

As we approach our journey of discovery to find what the real problem is here on earth, it is imperative that we begin with a context of truth that embodies all of the basic and fundamental principles of creation itself.

In order to understand creation, we must first understand the *source* of all creation, which is the very source of life itself. Here is where we run into a slight problem. There is no conceivable way that words alone can describe what this source is. The greatest mistake that human beings have made upon this planet is to believe that words and philosophical discussions can supply an adequate substitute for the missing experience of this source. In other words, if you can talk about it and even more so "believe" in it, then that is good enough. An experience is not really necessary, so many people believe, as long as you are prepared to agree that it does exist simply because some religion somewhere says so. As a matter of fact, the people of our world, in general, have come to believe that an experience of this source is in reality *unnecessary*, because we appear to be living just fine without it. But by whose standards? We might be alive, yes, but can we refer to the current global condition of humanity attempting to exist in so much pain, suffering, struggle, and destructiveness, as doing "just fine" without it? Is it possible that the *lack* of this experience is what's causing so much pain?

Then there are those who say that we are not even *worthy* of this experience, never mind deciding about whether or not it's necessary. They claim that our tendency to kill, harm, and destroy (sin, they call it) is living proof that we do not deserve any experience of love, life, or the source of anything. But what if we are actually performing these abominable acts (sins), as a *result* of not having this experience in the first place?

What if someone said to you, "You know, there is something called food, but *you* don't need it. Let's just talk about it. In fact, there's a guy who lived 2,000 years ago who tasted it once and people have been talking about it ever since! In fact, we can go over to this building over here and read menus about what food is like. That should be good enough for you. Just knowing it's there, somewhere, is all we really need."

So off you go to read the menus with a bunch of starving people. All skin and bones. But it's okay, because those menus are good enough for you!

Sound ridiculous? Well, maybe, but it is no different than believing that life can go on just fine without an experience of that which sources it. What do you suppose happens if you are alive in the midst of this powerful creation, that we call life, and don't have a single clue, experientially, of where it all comes from, where *you* came from, and how it all exists? In other words, you see it all before you, but you have no idea from where it comes. Do you believe that someone handing you a piece of paper with some words on it will somehow fix it all and then you'll know? Well let's try it and see if it works. Here are some wondrous, wonderful words for you: God, Love, Light, Omnipresence, Energy, and Infinite Intelligence. Can you write them on a piece of paper and say that you know? Can these words bring you salvation, fulfill you, and completely change your life for the better? If so, then let's write them on a sheet of paper, photocopy them 5½ billion times, pass them out to everyone, and the world will be saved tomorrow! No one will ever suffer again and every person alive will exist as a total manifestation of love, light, and truth. Amazing! Who would have thought it could be so easy?

By now, of course, some people will be thinking that this whole discussion is getting a bit out of hand and could we please get on with something more serious? But the truth is that it is a very serious matter when a planet full of people do not believe that it is necessary or important to have a full, dimensionally *real* experience of that which sources them and their life and are content to believe that words alone, which can be found in any dictionary, are an adequate substitute instead.

So with that in mind, let us proceed to discuss the source of creation and of life, while knowing full well that the words are not here to substitute for your experience.

There is a context of life that is so very real, so very pure and perfect, that it causes everything else to appear somewhat dim by comparison. This context is what we will refer to as the infinite source of all things that are real. The absolute nature of this source is that of love. Now this is not the sort of love that we are accustomed to thinking about in terms of how we live on this planetary earth. In other words, it is not on the level of love where we might arbitrarily say to someone, "I love you" or "you mean a lot to me," or things such as that. This is a love that is so profound, so completely awe-inspiring, that many have just barely touched it and instantly known that they could be one with that love.

This love is so pure, so infinite, that it is unspeakable in terms of its power to create life. Have you heard of the term "white light"? Where does it come from and how does it exist? A love that is so *clear* that it is impossible to comprehend, can only just be. It exists in a condition of no-time, or the eternal now, and is at one with its own manifestation. Its manifestation, from this point of the eternal now, is what we will call light and energy, although in truth they are one and the same. This light is no ordinary light. We are talking about a brilliance, a radiance, the brightness of which is unimaginable to the human mind, as we know it here. The energy that this light produces is so powerful that its potency is clearly infinite. There is no way to describe the presence of this love, the power with which it manifests as light and the resplendence by which it creates all things. It is simply beyond words and yet the experience of this power and presence exists at every moment, at every single level of life–at the level of molecules, atoms, your cells, your brain, your feeling heart and emotions. It is everywhere all at once. For this reason, we will refer to this love as Omnipresence. This omnipresent love, light, energy, power, and presence clearly exists in a radiating flow. That means, dear friends, that all of creation is also meant to function in that radiating flow as well.

As light slows down in frequency, which it does as it emanates further and further away from its actual source, it becomes recognizable as thought, or impulses of energy that spew outward from that source seeking to manifest further. So we can then say that thought is energy occurring at a frequency slower than light. In other words, it is light on its way to manifestation.

Picture, for a moment, a sun. Picture now the radiant brilliance of Omnipresence. See how the light travels outward from that central source and as it radiates its intensity appears to change. On a physical level of light, we would say that sunlight (which is in reality *starlight*) becomes more diminished as it radiates further away from its source. It dissipates because it spreads out more. This is a physical example. On the level of the ultimate source of life, the energetic frequency of that light becomes slower as it emanates and changes into the energy of thought impulses, which is a slower frequency of light. These thought impulses slow down even further and ultimately move into what we would call time and physical manifestation. The most important thing to remember is that the radiating power and energy of Omnipresence, love, light, thought, time, and physical manifestation are *one* continuum of the same energy which manifests at different levels of itself.

The rays of light which emanate from our sun remain the same sunlight from the same source regardless of the effect that is produced depending upon where it shines, reflects, and the distance from which these rays exist beyond the sun itself. Moonlight is really "sun" reflected off the moon. We can say it this way because a ray of sunlight is, in actuality, a piece of the sun itself. We "touch" the sun whenever we feel or see its light. The rays of the sun are not separate from the sun itself. They feel different from the core of that star, yet they are produced by that core and are a part of it nonetheless. So whenever you feel bathed in moonlight or bathed in the brilliant radiance of the sun itself, that star is upon you and you are experiencing it as directly as if you could touch it with your hand. In the light of our sun, you are touching the stars, and yet this is only a tiny example of something far more supreme and radiant.

Let us look now at the simple diagram on the next page. Diagram A demonstrates the way in which Omnipresence manifests itself as the whole of creation.

Of course this diagram is not to be taken literally, as a true manifestation of light into the physical does not happen in this linear way. But you can see in this picture how everything manifesting is, in actuality, an extension of Omnipresence. Creation is not separate from God, as many religions would have us believe, but *is* God.

Omnipresence is so powerful that it permeates everything because it *is* everything.

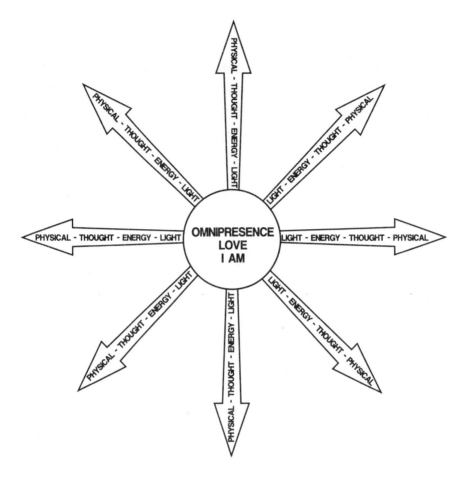

Diagram A

The intent of love that pervades all life is so powerful that it is truly an awesome thing to behold. If you could see the awesome nature of that intent and the uninterrupted power of that love, you would immediately recognize the truth, which is that you are one with it, and this would therefore become the basis for your whole reality.

It should be obvious by now that if everything exists as a manifestation of Omnipresence and its radiant core of bril-

40

liance, then indeed all creation exists, as well, in a radiating flow of that love. This means that everything in the Universe, including physical matter, is created in a radiating flow of energy and in fact *exists* as a radiating flow itself. That is why at the basis of *everything* you will find light. Perhaps this is what is meant by the "light of truth." It means that you have encountered the source, love, which is the truth behind all things. This is how we can say that ultimately we are love. It is not a matter of worthiness, you see, it is simply an undeniable scientific *fact*. We cannot change it. It is the only truth, the only reality. We are a manifestation of that love, that radiance and that divine energy; as we are a part of that same continuum. All that you need to do, to avoid feeling confused, is to simply recognize that there is something stopping your experience of that truth, which is why you can't feel it in full and why we appear to be so heavy and dense and negative in our world. Later on, we will explain what this word "negative" is really all about.

But for now, let us continue on with our explanation of Omnipresence and how that radiating power and brilliance generates all creation. If everything exists as a manifestation of Omnipresence and its radiant core of brilliance, which is love, then it would be fairly obvious that all things exist as well in a radiating flow of love. In other words, physical matter is created in a radiating flow of energy and in fact exists as a radiating flow of energy. That is why at the basis of everything you will find light. So with this premise we can no longer dispute the fact that life is made in a radiating flow. Try to remember this when we come to the chapter about reverse-flow and the Absence, so that you can truly comprehend the grave and devastating nature of a reverse-flow experience of life.

Now we are going to take a little bit of time here to begin a series of diagrams designed to represent the nature of creation and how it exists in the radiating flow of Omnipresence and Love. We will start by leaving the opposite page of this book (page 43) completely blank.

Imagine that this page represents infinity. Imagine that it has no borders, no boundaries, and no flat planes by which you can identify it. Imagine that it extends forwards, backwards, and on all sides in the infinite expansiveness of space. This page, we will say, represents Omnipresence. This blank page, and all that it represents in terms of infinity, will serve as the backdrop or context for our future diagrams about space, light, creation, and radiating flow.

Now let's go to page 44. On this page, we will add the words Omnipresence and Love. We will also draw some "points" or small dots to represent the points at which light changes to thought, and the impulse of energetic thought becomes a physical manifestation of something. Remember here that physical means *anything* that is a manifestation of light, and this definitely means things that are way beyond our microscopic experience in the overall physical, Inter-Universal spectrum of energy which is *huge* by comparison. We generally refer to our tiny part in that experience as being anything that we are able to measure via our five physical senses on this planetary earth.

So each dot represents the moment where thought becomes reality and therefore seeks its expression along that next continuum of reality in a radiating flow of expansion and evolution. Thus the universe is created and evolves.

From each of these points of reality, we will draw five arrows emanating from that point to demonstrate how creation exists in a radiating flow as it expands outwardly and becomes

OMNIPRESENCE
INFINITY

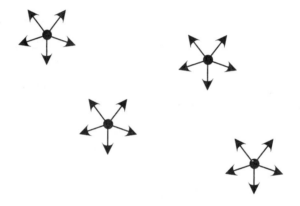

LOVE

Diagram B

more of itself. Let us now look at this next diagram, Diagram B on page 44, as we have described it so far.

Here we see each of these points of creation manifesting in a radiating flow of Love and Omnipresence. Each of these points could represent anything at all—planets, stars, moons, a flower, a molecule, an atom, or even a human being.

The important thing to note here is that the presence of each one contributes something to the surrounding whole, as shown by the arrows moving outward in a radiating flow of that presence.

Every one of these elements of creation exists as a statement of "I am" something. Ultimately, they exist as a statement of "I am Omnipresence." They are each an individual, unique expression of Omnipresence itself, or put another way, a *presence* of who they are.

Let's now add this final element of "I am" to our diagram to complete our visual model of these very simple aspects of creation. Look now at Diagram C on page 46.

In this final drawing, we see the power of simple presence and how everything in creation ultimately exists as a statement and manifestation of "I am Omnipresence," "I am Infinity" and "I am Love."

All of these individual entities express themselves as love into the surrounding space and therefore integrate perfectly with the rest of creation. How does this integration occur? Behind the entire cosmos, Omnipresence manifests as Infinite Intelligence or creative energy and thereby creates a blueprint of life and the entire cosmos as One Thought, One Plan, and One Outcome which is the fullest possible manifestation of Love, Light, and evolution. Every single element of creation contains within itself this blueprint of that One Thought of which it is a part, which allows it to exist in total harmony

OMNIPRESENCE
INFINITY

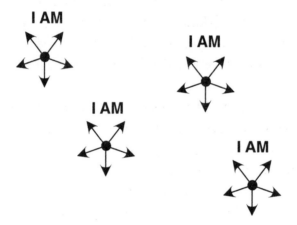

LOVE

Diagram C

with everything else. You could say that that One Thought exists holographically within every, single thing.

And the final thing to note is this. Each of these elements of creation, each individual manifestation of Omnipresence, is backed by the entire whole of the Universe and everything in it and by Omnipresence itself, which means that each and every individual is ultimately an expression of the greater whole. In other words, the greater whole of life is experiencing and expressing itself through the existence of every individual thing that exists within it.

This ultimately means that a state of oneness exists throughout the Universe. In that oneness, we will find ourselves, which is Omnipresence.

Let us now see what happens when a group of space travelers encounter our earth for the very first time in this experience of Oneness!

Chapter 5

Our Planet in Space

The only perspective from which to approach the final elimination of the source of fear is from the perspective of global evolution or the evolution of our earth. This is the only context that is large enough to allow us to eliminate the entire problem, once and for all, instead of only dealing with the symptoms.

In the cosmos itself, we find an interdimensional reality of thought, which is a product of Infinite Intelligence manifesting itself as creation in space. This creation is supremely beautiful and the experience of passing through the stars, the planets, and all life is the ultimate in serenity, harmony, peace, and letting go. It is from a place of surrender and oneness that we have a chance to experience the sublime creation of the Universe itself. What some have called *space*.

In this space reside all of the stars and planets, including our earth. Let us now create a scenario in our minds eye where a group of space travelers encounter our earth for the first time. We will create them to be a more advanced version of ourselves and definitely without any such problem as the source of fear. In other words, these travelers in space exist as gods. What does it mean to be a god? A god is a human being who exists in the fullest presence of who they are. There is no interruption in their radiating flow of energy and they exist fully and completely as a manifestation of Omnipresence in human form.

Now for some people this might sound like a "bit too much." How can anyone possibly consider a human being to be a god?

"That's ridiculous," some might say. Do you remember what we said in the last chapter about worthiness? It's not a matter of being worthy, as though being a god is a title or something you would try to live up to. The truly ridiculous thing is that we believe it's a matter of worthiness rather than a simple matter of science. We might as well ask if a rose is worthy to be a rose, or if a star is worthy to be a star. Do you think a grass-hopper is worthy to be a grasshopper or should it have to live up to that title first?

The reason that we refer to human beings in full presence as gods is because we as our true selves possess the same cre-ative capabilities as God itself. Does that sound like blasphemy? Only if you think that God is separate and that we are in some kind of competition with that God in terms of who is ultimately in "control" of the Universe. To say that we are *not* God is the ultimate level of ego, control, and separation. In a short period of time, you are going to find out exactly why that is. You are also going to find out why we are so afraid to admit that we are God and Omnipresence manifesting in a form that we call human, and why we find that idea to be so threatening that we run from it in fear. We then rationalize our running away and justify our fear by saying that we are just not worthy of the "title." Well, dear friends, it is not a title. It is not some-thing that you artificially slap on your head like some special "seal of approval" which says that you are okay in spite of your dysfunctional actions. If those dysfunctional actions are there, it means that something is most definitely impeding the radiant flow and presence of who you truly are, and causing you to do strange things and think strange thoughts in the wake of that impediment. Whatever is impeding that power-ful flow and expression of Omnipresence attempting to mani-fest through you in a radiating flow of love (which is what it does throughout the entire Universe with *everything*—not just humans), is what's causing you to look amazingly foolish and dumb to yourself and therefore simultaneously causing you to say as well, "Who me? Omnipresence? Ha! No way! You must be crazy."

But at any rate, let's go back to our space travelers who are awaiting our wondrous description of them so that they can leap into being in our minds eye. These travelers are human, to be sure, but they exist only in a radiating presence of love. From that power that pours through them, and is simultaneously who they are, they experience oneness with the entire Universe and from that place are able to explore everything in harmony, peace, and with an abundant appreciation of life itself. They are also able to create. But they are not creators of just anything, with no regard for how it fits in with the rest of the cosmos. They are creators of life, planets, stars, and even galaxies! How can they do this? Do they just snap their fingers and "zap" them into being? Of course not. What they do in reality is play a co-creative role with the Universe itself and all of the forces of Nature and evolution, and simply do their part in the greater scheme of things to create what is ultimately the great cosmos of life.

Their creative abilities are so far superior to ours that by comparison it looks as though we are only using some tiny, microscopic portion of our brains. And even with that tiny bit, we are still using a large portion of that tiny part to destroy things. Ourselves included. But how can they be human and possess such massive power? Because, dear friends, the "massive power" is not theirs to possess. The massive power, per se, does not belong to them. On the contrary, it flows *through* them and therefore exists as an expression of who they are. Have you ever heard a quotation from one of the greatest beings who ever lived upon this planetary sphere called earth? I believe it was something like "I and my Father are one and the same." What do you think that means? Do you think it means, "I am and you're not"? Now, many people would dispute the "Father" part as being sexist. We would simply say that it's incomplete. But we can never be sure what that entity *really* said in terms of an exact quote and choice of words. After all, we have a tough time getting a story straight just passing it around among a small circle of friends. Can you imagine an actual, real quote being preserved with perfect integrity and flawless, tape-recorder precision from 2,000 years ago (when there were no tape-recorders) when it's been told and retold *millions* of times, translated and retranslated who knows how often, and passed around all over the place for two full millenniums? But regardless of the words, we can certainly get the meaning, which of course is spoken in the highest truth of what it is to be a human being. In short, what this entity is simply saying is, "I am Omnipresence." Do you think that this person existed on this earth to say to everyone, "I am a human being, and you're *not*"? or to say, "I am a physical manifestation of supreme light, love, power, and divine energy and *you*, unfortunately, will never have a chance of being that yourself. Too bad for you!" Of course such words were never spoken, nor were they intended. But we *behave* almost as though they were! We relentlessly hold onto an attitude that this incredible being was truly the fullest embodiment of God itself and yet we insist on retaining a collective belief that we, even 2,000 years later, are still the same lowly sinners and rotten, miserable, unworthy creatures as we were 2,000 years ago when he was here. We haven't moved an inch! How can you love someone, such as Yeshua, or Jesus, as some have called him, and yet give no indication that his powerful presence on this planet had any meaning in *your* life except to firmly verify that yes, you are indeed the wretched, wrong creature that you always thought you were. That would be like saying to someone who had devoted themselves, for your benefit, to helping you see the tremendous beauty in yourself and then saying to that person, "Thank you very much for all of your effort. It has had exactly the opposite effect that you intended it to have. I have taken your most powerful and beautiful inspiration and used it to confirm my own ugliness. Thanks!"

So let's go back to our space travelers, who by now are wondering where we are and if we are still intending to pursue this journey with them. Hopefully by now we have put the unworthiness issue to rest and can fully allow them to be who they are in the context of our limited reality.

So these entities are bright and beautiful gods who reside in the Universe and have among themselves the most *incredible* space vessel that you have ever imagined in your wildest dreams! It is all white and brilliantly radiant against the black, velvet backdrop of infinite space and its all-consuming silence. Do you know what the silence in space really is? It is the space within which Omnipresence resides. It is so profound that it is almost tangible. That silence will move you to the core of your being and is overwhelming in terms of its infinite nature and power. It is that which cradles life. All life, in every form.

So this beautiful, brilliant ship with its wondrous crew and radiant energy passes among the stars, unnoticed, as it gracefully transits the unbelievable power and awesome presence of an Omnipresent mind. This is space, which is indeed the final frontier.

Our ship's captain and crew are busy going about their business, which on this vessel involves a random exploration of space within a certain parameter of our galaxy. The interesting thing about this ship and its wondrous crew is that they are not confined to one dimension of time and space as we are here in our world. They have the capability of existing interdimensionally and traveling interdimensionally as well. This comes in very handy for long journeys through the Universe, where attempting to travel along our space-time continuum within which earth resides would take so long that everyone would be dead before they could even leave their own galaxy. So these wondrous travelers and their illustrious ship could actually exist right above us and we wouldn't even know it because they would be in another dimension! Amazing!

At any rate, in the first part of our journey they are not exactly above us, but somewhere in the neighboring vicinity in another Universe, or other dimension of reality, collecting rock specimens from various planets that they have recently seeded with life. At this point in our experience of them, they are simply gliding silently through space and engaging in some relaxed and friendly banter among themselves, as they proceed toward their next destination.

All of a sudden the ship's entire system is jolted out of its graceful movement with a piercing sound and the cry of, "Red Alert!" The crew is shocked and momentarily dazed for they have never experienced anything quite like this before. They quickly collect themselves, drop everything, and rush to their respective emergency positions on the bridge and throughout the ship.

The captain, a great being of power, strength, and grace, sits at the helm, poised to give an instant command as information starts flooding in from all of the ship's systems, via computer, to be translated by various officers who are manning their posts.

The ship seems to be vibrating at a strange and unusual frequency, one that is unrecognizable to the people on board, but clearly very dangerous. The captain quickly orders the ship to move out of range of this strange vibration, which the crew immediately handles by transferring the ship to a nearby, alternate dimension. The ship has now actually "disappeared" from its previous location and interdimensionally entered another time and space. From this new location, they are able to collect additional data about their strange encounter without being negatively affected by it. They can do this because this incredible ship possesses a special interdimensional sensing intelligence that is capable of spanning a wide range of realities, specifically any of the ones that they are able to enter into. Each of these realities or dimensions of creation are identified by vibrational sound, which affords them the utmost, flawless precision in homing in on any particular world. By homing in to the particular sound vibration of any specific dimension of life, the ship and crew, via super-advanced technology are able to vibrate in sympathetic attunement with that dimension, enter into it, and thereby become a part of it for as long as they wish. You might have guessed that their physical bodies are immortal, yet they are physically affected by whatever time-continuum of thought that they might enter into and must always take this into consideration during the course of their travels. Yet their physical command over their bodies' vibrational frequency, via thought waves and energetic nervous impulses, is an awesome thing to behold and is what affords them the widest possible range of expression throughout their immortal Universe.

So now that everyone is relaxed in their new post in space, the captain begins to ask questions. "What do you make of it?" he asks the first officer who is quietly performing a simulation test on the ships computer based on data that they have just received.

"Fascinating," says the first officer. "It appears, captain, that we have encountered a strange, alien energy emanating from somewhere in this nearby sector of the galaxy."

"What do you mean 'alien'?" asks the captain.

"Alien, captain, refers to some particular thought form existing in opposition to life."

"But that's impossible! Nothing can be against life. *Everything* is life. Everything is presence. And might I remind you, as well, that everything is One."

"Yes, captain, but nonetheless it *is* happening."

"Let me see," replies the captain as he moves over to the screen where his first officer has been assessing their situation. "Amazing!" He turns to the science officer, "can you get me the sound coordinates from where this frequency is sourced?"

"I already have it," says the science officer. "Look here. It appears to be coming from the third planet in this particular solar system."

"What is the name of that planet?" asks the captain.

"Captain," says the first officer, "the planet is referred to as 'earth' by its human inhabitants."

"There are humans on that planet? My god! What sort of condition are they in?"

"I am unable to tell," responds the first officer. "This 'thing' appears to have produced a void around the planet that makes it impossible to see what is happening there from where we are."

"What are we going to do?" asks the science officer. "There is no way to see what is happening on that planet because the people are existing in total separation from the rest of the Universe."

The captain walks away with his head down, thinking quietly. "There must be a way," he says. "We can't just leave them there."

The ships navigator pipes up, "Well, there is one way, captain. But it's not very safe."

"What way is that?" responds the captain.

"We could enter into a dimension which is very close to that one, where enough of an influence can be felt by our ships sensors to give us an opportunity to track the energy down onto the planet itself and provide us with enough of a 'window' to see what is going on. The problem is that by following that influence, we don't know how we ourselves might be affected."

The captain turns again to his first officer, "Do you know of any way that we might protect ourselves from this alien influence?"

"Well, captain, suppose that we remain in union with the truth and approach this planet with an intention to serve and right the situation once again. It might just be enough to keep us from being overly affected."

The captain wipes his brow and thinks silently for a moment. "All right, we'll do it. Surely this thing can't be that powerful if it functions in a way that is against life and the entire Universe. How powerful can something be which functions alone?"

He resumes his position at the helm and issues an immediate command for the ship's entry into a neighboring dimension where the ship's sensors will be able to home in on this alien vibration and open a window for them to see what's going on.

Let's pause here for a moment to say something about the nature of this ship. Unlike the technologies that we are accustomed to on our planet, this ship is not made of metal, per se, but rather is designed as living, vibrational matter which can respond to human thought and hold many different frequencies of energy, depending upon the needs of the crew. In this case, the captain orders that the ship and all crew members hold within their consciousness the highest possible vibration of Love in the current form that they are in.

They are now ready to open their dimensional "window" and witness what is going on. First, the ship homes in on the alien frequency. The crew members are feeling a strange sensation throughout their cells as their molecules become affected by this unusual vibration. They immediately enter into a state of ill health as their bodies become deprived of a certain amount of life force. Their thoughts begin to cloud and each person starts to feel a peculiar "gripping" sensation around their heart. It is painful. The captain immediately realizes that they will not be able to stay here for very long. He orders a series of "information shots" taken from around the planet, a holographic "picture-taking" capability included in the ship's amazing repertoire of functions. The amazing thing about this particular capability is that the ships holographic "camera" can expand in earth's time and literally photograph huge blocks of time and all of the accompanying activities in a matter of seconds! The captain orders this particular technology because in this way they will be there for the shortest amount of time and can observe the results from a safer distance.

Now that they have their required data, they move to a safer zone to study the evidence. The captain calls his closest officers into a committee room, while the rest of the crew members immerse themselves in the task of returning all of the ship's frequencies back to normal. The last officer closes the door behind her and everyone takes a seat around a circular "vision area" in the center of the room, where the ship's systems will play for them a holographic "movie" of whatever it recorded on planet earth. The lights are dimmed. Everyone sits silently and awaits with bated breath as the captain issues the command, "Begin."

What they witness is so profoundly horrifying that it brings forth emotion and tears from a place within themselves where they have never felt such things.

"My God, captain, they're killing each other," whispers the first officer in a state of shock and disbelief. The captain wipes a tear from his cheek while powerful emotions well up inside of him from a deep, core place of truth.

"They're starving! There's no food!" exclaims the navigation officer as she observes the poverty and hunger that reigns over much of the planet.

"Captain, look! They're killing the trees and destroying the very biosystems of the planet that they depend on for life with dangerous chemicals and poisons. This is madness!" cries someone else.

"Yes," the captain states quietly. "They have all gone completely mad."

The science officer steps up to the viewing circle for a closer look. "Captain," he says, "let's read their thoughts."

The captain agrees and orders the ship's computer to vibrationally transfer their thought fields from their brains (because this "camera" records *everything*), translate it via sound into a language which the crew can understand and display it vibrationally in the center of the circle where everyone present can see into the minds of these strangely affected peoples. What they see is even more shocking than the behavior they have just witnessed.

"Captain," exclaims a nearby communications officer, "all of their thoughts are *against* themselves!"

"Yes," says the captain, "I believe they call it doubt."

"A more appropriate word would be 'hate'," replies the first officer.

"Hate? What is hate?" asks the captain as he turns to his closest comrade.

"Hatred is a word that best describes a total reversal of human intelligence, where the human mind attempts to function in total detachment from the Universe without benefit of any impulse of truth. The resulting division causes such a mind to appear separate, almost as though it were a singular entity unto itself. Such a mind becomes tiny and out of reacting to the void within which it exists, it proceeds to bark angry, small orders back to the human who exists in ownership of it. These orders generally take on a tone of being *against* someone or something, but most usually manifests in a tone of being against the bearer of the mind."

"Fascinating!" says the captain. "This thing appears to have cut off huge portions of their intelligence!"

"And their hearts, too," points out a small woman seated toward the back. "As the ship's Universal Overseer, I have been fascinated to observe what is happening with these people emotionally."

"Yes," says another communications officer, "it appears that in many ways they are no longer able to feel."

"Well, how else could they perform all of these abominable acts?" replies the captain. "They are literally destroying themselves!"

"Captain," the first officer states, "it appears that these people have been dramatically affected by this alien influence in such a way that they are turning against themselves. They have little or no regard for themselves, each other, and life itself. They are basically living in a downward spiral, hell-bent on self-destruction."

"But that goes completely against what it means to be human!" states another science officer, as he reflects on the power and beauty of his own situation in life.

"Yes," says the first officer, "but you see these people don't know any longer what a human being is. They have misdefined themselves and believe that they *are* their wretched situation."

"Do you mean to say that they believe that they are an actual life form whose design it is to perform these horrific actions?" asks a communication officer.

"Exactly," replies the first officer. "They think that because they do these things, and because they have no experience of anything else due to the fact that they are completely cut off from the Universe, that this is all there is and have therefore identified human existence as their own desperate struggle to survive in the wake of their own self-destruction."

"So they are living completely in a void," replies the captain.

"In a manner of speaking, yes."

The captain stands up and orders the ship's computer to turn off the viewing circle. Everyone sits quietly as they solemnly watch the empty space before them where the viewing circle has just finished playing for them the incredible human situation on planet earth.

"What could have caused such a terrifying situation on this planet, captain?" asks an officer who was previously silent.

"I don't know," responds the captain, "but we are going to find out."

Chapter 6

Time: Real and Artificial

Our space travelers are now preparing to collect new data as to the actual source of the problem on planet earth. This is very tricky, however, because in order to locate the source, they will have to discover a way for the ship's computer to access that source without negatively affecting the ship.

The captain observes the space-time continuum within which earth resides. "Hmmm," he says. "This alien force appears to have found its entryway along earth's continuum of space/time reality."

"Well," says the first officer, "then that is where we will have to go in order to track it and find its source."

"I don't think so," says the captain. "If we move into their continuum of space/time reality, then we, too, will become a part of it and I don't see any way in which to do that without becoming affected by it."

"That's right." says the science officer. "Then we would find it impossible to be objective, just like the people on earth. Like them, there is a chance that we, too, might actually fall prey to the belief that this alien force is a part of us as well."

"But how is that possible?" asks the Universal Overseer. "It is so clear that it is a force *against* life. How could it possibly be interpreted as human or anything else that is real?"

The science officer explains, "This alien force of energy has found a way to reverse the magnetic field of consciousness that embodies each and every human being and brings them into existence. This means that all of their thoughts, feelings, and emotions tend to occur in reverse. Thus their activities are designed to be repressed and self-destructive rather than expanded and life-enhancing." He goes on to explain further. "Because their magnetic field exists in a state of reversal, they interpret that reversed field of energy to still be their own. Unfortunately, this thing also has the power to blind them and render them basically unconscious to the truth. Because they can't see it, to them it doesn't exist. All that exists is their own current situation."

"But how can they live this way and still survive?" ask another officer.

"They are not doing a very good job of it," continues the science officer. "They exist in a state of tremendous despair because in their heart of hearts, they *know* that what they're experiencing cannot be the truth. Yet, they have lost their ability to see and to feel in the real sense of Love. So what they do instead is to engage some very basic, primitive survival mechanisms on an emotional level. They basically have to *convince* themselves that all of this is just fine and the way in which nature intended it."

"Do you mean that they *lie* to themselves?" asks another communications officer who is keenly interested in the whole discussion.

"That's exactly what I mean," replies the science officer. "You see, they have no choice. If they can't see the truth, then indeed they have no hope. They would therefore find it difficult or impossible to survive the emotionally crushing nature of their situation. In order to cope with that reality and go on living, they must *convince* themselves that this is indeed how 'God' intended it."

"God? What is that word God?" asks someone else.

The first officer answers, "The word 'God' is a word that was developed over time to describe the experience of Omnipresence and Love, which they are no longer feeling in their hearts. They know it is there, but are unable to experience it because this alien force of energy has completely arrested their experience of who they are. The way in which they compensate for this missing experience is by gathering together in various orders of thought which they have institutionalized into something they call 'religion'."

"Religion? What's that?" asks another.

"Religion," says the captain, "is when a group of these people get together to talk about an experience of life which they do not have."

"But how can they talk about an experience that they don't have?" asks the officer in charge of radiant light communications.

"That's just it. They don't," replies the captain. "They read very old books about someone else who has had the experience, elect a certain few official-types to interpret it, and then dispense the rules and regulations of that interpretation to the masses."

"But that's insanity!" exclaims another.

"Yes it is, dear friends, but it's all that they have. They figure that if they can at least talk about it, then that gives them some remains of a thread which might connect them to the Universe and keep them feeling as though they have a life line to reality."

"So what happens if these interpretations don't match?" asks another. "How do they all manage to agree on something that they don't experience for themselves?"

"That's just it," says the captain. "Usually they don't. The religions actually end up killing people sometimes as tremendous battles and power struggles ensue over whose interpretation is the 'right' one."

"Do you mean to say that certain religions have actually murdered other human beings who don't agree with what they have to say about *life*? That's impossible!" chuckles another officer who finds the whole thing so unbelievable that he would like to dismiss the entire discussion right now.

"Not impossible in these people's situation," says the captain. "Remember that their entire consciousness has been reversed, so they therefore see life and freedom as the enemy. In their minds, control and repression are the only way to survive."

"Are you saying that they no longer have faith and trust in the Universe?" asks someone else.

"How can they have faith in something which they do not experience?" answers the captain. "To them, life is now their enemy and they are attempting to survive in *spite* of it."

"My god, it must be an incredibly lonely existence for each and every one of them," says another woman officer who has been patiently listening to the entire discussion.

"Yes it is," says the captain, "but they don't ever admit that to anyone. They usually try to keep it hidden inside of themselves. In fact, their sense of aloneness is so profound that they tend to look for every opportunity to distract themselves from the pain of that experience. They try to make sure that no one else knows about it, because to admit to that would be overwhelmingly impossible to cope with. Their greatest coping mechanism is for everyone to do their best to pretend that everything is 'just fine'."

Everyone pauses for a few moments as the officers contemplate the emotional severity of the human situation in this strange and unusual planetary dilemma.

"Enough," says the captain. "We will transcend their space/ time continuum, and position ourselves in the Universal Arc of Timelessness where we can allow the ship's sensors to get a full reading on the nature of whatever phenomenon is causing all of this trouble."

"But it will be very difficult to find the exact coordinates which will allow us to do that, captain," says the ship's chief engineer. "The Arc of Timelessness is an incredibly broad spectrum of reality!"

"Well," says the captain with a smile, "let's just approach it as something new and the forces of life and creation will no doubt provide us with a way."

While our illustrious space crew is busy developing their new strategy for acquiring the needed information about the source of the problem on planet earth, let's you and I take a break from them for a moment and discuss our own particular notions of time and space as they exist on our planet.

Real Time

Let us first talk about real time. In order to understand real time, we must begin in the place from which time itself originates. Ironically, the place from which to begin experiencing and understanding time is the eternal now, where there is no time.

What is the eternal now? It is quite simply the space within which everything resides. In terms of the Universe, it is the infinite space which holds all of the planets, stars, galaxies, and every interstellar phenomenon that exists. It is what holds life. It is from the Now that everything is created.

Many times people will make an effort to have a real experience of this eternal Now for themselves as a spiritual pursuit or path of meditation. Yet you can actually witness the existence of this Now by simply looking up into the night sky and observing the space between the stars. That infinite blackness of space indicates, as we said earlier, the Presence within which all things exist.

That Presence of space is, as well, what cradles the existence of your own human body. Many times people have wondered how they might be able to have a physical, mental, and emotional experience of this eternal now. It seems impossible on the surface, because it appears that we are so caught up in time.

Yet the tiny atoms which comprise your physical, human body are held and suspended within exactly the same space as this Now which holds the awesome physical forces of the Universe in the form of planets, stars, and huge interstellar phenomena. All thought, including thoughts about time, are generated from the Now. And feelings are experienced within this same context of Now, as well. All things reside within this space of Now. This space, this oneness, is the context for everything and exists as the infinite backdrop for the relative relationship between objects in space which is what produces time.

In other words, you have infinite space, that fabric of one thing which is ultimately Omnipresence, which holds within itself everything in creation. In this fabric of oneness you will find the ultimate continuum that crosses *everything*, and provides our space travelers with the flexibility to traverse so many different dimensions and realities. Because they are aware of the oneness of this continuum and how it pervades all things, they are able to center themselves here and then "step" from one reality to the next, from one dimension to the next, in space, much like a child stepping on different stones to cross a stream of running water. In a similar way, they use these different realities and dimensions of time to "step" very efficiently across the Universe and reach their various destinations in a most proficient way. All that they have to understand is how one reality connects to the next and then the next and then the next. It goes on and on, as all realities are ultimately interwoven in the same interdimensional, interstellar, inter-Universal tapestry of space, which is what we finally call creation itself.

Many times people are fond of referring to space as "inner space" or "outer space." But the truth is, there is only one space. Until you recognize this, you will not be able to know or experience what we mean by this eternal Now. If you just use simple logic, however, you will be halfway there. If we can reiterate one more time—all things, all dimensions, and all experiences ultimately take place within the same space. That space is the Oneness which cradles everything in a condition known as no-time. From this place, we can experience our human presence and who we truly are. It is the foundation of empowerment, insight, foresight, and incredible creative capability. But ultimately, it is the center for peace and an infinite knowing of how all things exist.

Let's now talk about time itself. Real time exists within the Now. Real time has to do with the relative relationship of one thing to another in space. Ultimately, an experience of real time in space means to be in tune with the powerful intergalactic, interplanetary, interstellar rhythms of the spheres which we commonly call the celestial bodies in space. There are an infinite number of possible real-time scenarios in space, depending upon the reality and the dimension within which one exists. For purposes of our understanding, however, we will speak only of real time as it pertains to our experience here on planet earth.

Our primary experience of real time here centers on the relationship of our planet to its mother star, the sun. The sun is the center of our solar system, and therefore the center of how we we perceive time. To keep it simple, let us say that our most natural experience of real time occurs when we feel our bodies to be in tune with the natural rhythms of our planet, the sun, the solar system, and the galaxy. We are not able to identify what all of these rhythms are, yet identification is not really necessary because our bodies are naturally in tune with these rhythms magnetically. Everything in the Universe is held together magnetically. Thoughts are magnetic and it is thought which ultimately produces the fabric of creation. So being in tune is a magnetic phenomenon. Because of the magnetic interconnectedness of all things as one great thought manifesting as the power of Infinite Intelligence, we already exist in tune with stars, planets, and galaxies that we may not even know exist on a conscious level. We are a part of the great intergalactic rhythms in space.

Isn't it wonderful that we, as humans, don't have to be able to identify *everything* in order for Nature to work?

So let us look next at what produces these powerful rhythms of Nature. The answer is movement. Everything in creation moves in relationship to everything else. This is true for everything in the cosmos. All things are interconnected, because all things move together in one great dance. To be in harmony means to be magnetically connected to this Universal, cosmic dance in such a way that you experience surrender to whatever is your part in that dance. This is not something that you can control, because it is Omnipresence which is behind the whole thing. It is that which creates all things and gives rise to the entire creation, of which we, too, are a part.

So in surrender we will experience real time. We start with an experience of the Now, the place from which our presence and all true experiences are sourced. From there we experience our interconnectedness with all things in the Universe, and most specifically our galaxy. Because we are earth beings we will be most aware of the special rhythms of our planet as they pertain to the sun, the central star in our solar system. These rhythms manifest in waves and produce beautiful sound frequencies which can be heard throughout the cosmos. The rhythm of day into night, the rhythm of the seasons, the rhythm of the earth's graceful orbit around the sun, the rhythm of all of our neighboring planets flowing in great arcs and circles together around our central sun and the unison of all of these powerful movements, the rhythms of the many creatures that inhabit the earth, which are in tune with the greater solar rhythms of our tiny star system in space, the rhythms of plants, the rhythms of the moon, the singing rhythms of all of the moons in our system of planets, the perfection and interwoven nature of all of these celestial, space rhythms even within our tiny solar system, are absolutely gorgeous to behold and to experience. The coexistence of all of these natural rhythms in perfect balance is truly the ultimate demonstration of harmony.

In truth, real time is music. It is movement that is represented by the relative positioning of all things as they change in relationship to one another and therefore emit sound. Everything emits sound, as in truth, everything vibrates in order to exist. Real time is witnessed in the rhythm, cycles, and the unseen music produced by the spheres as they move and undulate in the great and powerful cycles produced by Nature. The beauty of real time can be experienced in day and night, seasons, cycles, rhythms, planetary orbits and rotations, and ultimately in galactic time and seasons of which we know not. Ultimately, real time is represented by the entire interstellar space/time continuum within which we witness the interweaving of multitudinous dimensions of life and creation.

And finally, there is evolutionary time which is the great and powerful timing of evolution itself. We exist in One powerful Universe which is evolving itself in response to the awesome forces of Nature and Omnipresence. We, on our tiny, tiny planet, are no exception to that evolution. We are a part of it and in that part are connected to the whole.

The only thing that one can ultimately say about real time is that it must be experienced in order to be known. We must live in a state of surrender and completely let go to our presence and our existence in Love. In that surrender, we will then experience real time via our magnetic connection to all things in life, which on a physical level happens even on the micro, sub-atomic levels of our own human bodies. We are completely connected, to be sure, and the way in which to experience that connection is to let go completely and allow ourselves and our bodies to come back in tune with the Universe as a whole. Surrender is the key to the entire experience. In experiencing real time, we ultimately experience oneness with the Universe and realize the truth, which is that nothing is separate.

Artificial Time

In our world, where the source of fear exists, we find ourselves unable or unwilling, out of fear, to surrender completely to the forces of Nature. We therefore do not experience real time, and cannot experientially connect with the magnificent and beautiful rhythms of our entire cosmos, earth included. We find ourselves unable to be a part of this magnificent symphony of Universal time and space and our bodies and consciousness therefore become askew and unable to perform in a natural way. We find ourselves unable to evolve normally, because our whole systems exist in a state of physical, mental, and emotional arrest. In short, we are out of sync, out of step, out of alignment, and out of tune with Nature, with ourselves, and with the cosmos at large. We therefore attempt to compensate for this by engaging all manner of controlling behavior in some misguided attempt to "get a hold" of ourselves and fix the problem.

One of our most blatant attempts to control life, ourselves, and our personal and collective evolution is through the invention of artificial time.

Artificial time is firmly rooted in an act of division and the cold, calculated "measuring" of some of the beautiful rhythms that we described earlier. When we, as a species, found ourselves separated, as a result of the source of fear, from these intense and beautiful rhythms of life we were immediately disconnected from the Universe and found ourselves in a state of panic and survival at a very primordial level. We then perceived ourselves to be basically alone and expected to function completely on our own, so we perceived to be the truth in our separated state. Thus we tried to "grab on" to our perception of these orbital cycles and rhythms and somehow control them in such a way that we would be able to *artificially* connect with them, since we were unable to do it naturally any longer. This panic occurred as we found ourselves unable to surrender, which is the only way to experience real time. Faith, surrender, and an experience of real time are what allow us to be fully who we are and evolve powerfully and consciously in the realm of Universal consciousness. But we had no faith any longer, because we were disconnected and alone. So we thought.

Thus, out of this fear, aloneness, and absolute lack of faith in Nature and the Universe which we could no longer see, we became compelled to understand our reality and thereby control ourselves, by measuring it through artificial means.

The artificial method by which we measure the powerful cycles of earth and creation is through the use of clocks and calendars.

Let's start with the clock. The inventing of our clock is based upon the concept of division. (Which is interesting, since this whole idea came out of our experience of separation.) A clock is like a giant ruler, in the shape of a sphere, which we place over the top of our planet and use to measure the rotation of our earth.

Look at the following diagram, to see how this works.

Our clock appears conceptually as a giant cage placed over our planet, with 24 bars. Each of these bars exists to mark every "hour" of time. An hour, in truth, equals a certain physical distance on the planet itself which is what "time zones" are all about.

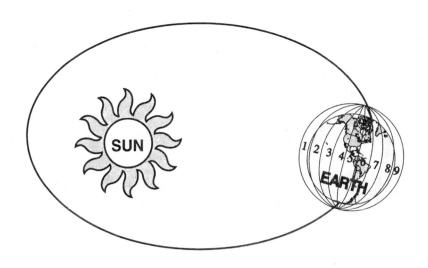

Diagram A

Imagine yourself standing at point "X" on our planet. There you are, minding your own business, just enjoying the beautiful experience of life, rhythm, and nature, when all of a sudden you look up into the sky and realize that earth is rotating inside of a giant jail cell! You count the bars as you pass underneath each one and come up with a total of 24. You immediately jump up, run to the telephone, and phone up your friend who lives in another part of the world. Very excitedly you explain, "Have you seen what I've just seen? We're in a cage! The earth is in a cage!"

Your friend responds, "A cage? That's impossible. How could we be in a cage?"

You say, "Go look outside. You'll see the bars. Count them for yourself."

So, your friend goes outside and just at that moment a huge bar passes overhead with the number "11" printed on it. Way off in the distance, he notices another bar emerge from over the horizon with the number "12". And in between each of these bars are a series of smaller bars, all numbered consecutively from 1 to 60. "My gosh!" he exclaims and runs back into the house to pick up the phone. "You're right!" he says. "We're trapped! Trapped in space! Our earth is definitely in a jail."

What you have both figured out by now is that depending on which bar your little spot on the planet is passing under as it rotates, the number on that bar indicates for you precisely what "time" it is where you stand.

Sound ludicrous? Well, dear friends, this is the *truth* of how we live. Maybe we can't run outside and *see* those bars, per se, but they most definitely exist in all of our minds as though they were completely, irrevocably real.

Now here's the next most fascinating thing about this game called artificial time. In artificial time, we tell ourselves that we *must* do certain things by the time our little spot on the planet passes underneath certain bars. We must eat at certain "times" (under certain bars). We must sleep at certain "times" (also under certain bars). Does anyone ever look at the light of day, feel the rhythm of our planetary rotation as that day moves into night, watch the disappearing light and energy of our star, as our part of the earth rotates away from that light giving us a chance to experience the mystical, awesome power of deep space and the presence and light of other, more distant stars, and watch how that awesome movement of our planetary sphere affects our bodies, relaxes us, and induces sleep? No, of course not. We go immediately to a *clock*, a miniature model of our giant, imaginary cage, find out what bar we're at and go by the rules of the bar, which is the *only* thing which dictates sleep. Whether it's day or night is irrelevant to us. The clock is the only thing that matters.

Now we are not suggesting that you throw away your clocks. Perhaps they are useful as time coordinates in our exceedingly artificial world. But please, if you use them, see them for what they are, and don't imagine them to be some very necessary element in nature, because they're not. How often do we become frustrated because nature does not respond in any way to our "clock rules" and doesn't even recognize that they exist? How many a doctor has become angry that the awesome power of a woman's labor in childbirth did not correspond to the artificial clock and follow the clock rules, which say that every single baby *must* come out by such and such a time according to the clock? What's wrong with nature? Didn't nature give those babies watches? Well, no matter. The clock rules all and if those babies don't arrive *on time*, then we'll just say that nature is wrong. Because everyone knows that nature does not dictate the awesome power of birth. The clock does! Perhaps we should make altars for our clocks and place them there, because to us they must be our only god if we are willing to yank babies out of their mothers bodies in all sorts of horrendous ways just to get them here "on time." We don't even believe those babies have a chance to survive if they don't come out "by the clock." That's how much we think our life depends on it.

Can you imagine trying to birth a baby "by the clock?" Why do you think medical science has to intervene so much? It is solely for the purpose of artificially forcing that baby and its birth to squeeze into the time constraints of the clock. No wonder parents are so nervous. "Oh God! What if my baby doesn't fit? We can't trust nature. Nature is too unpredictable. It's scary. Let's get that baby out any way we can! As long as it fits with the clock, we'll know we're safe. We'll even cut it out, if necessary! Whew! What a relief. Made it. Just in time!"

Now, for those of you who are jumping up and down shouting, "But what about medical emergencies?" Please. We are not being foolish. But how many of these so-called emergencies are actually due to the restraining environment of the clock-rules, which make it impossible for any woman to connect with the awesome forces of Nature (which in truth really do birth the baby), and thereby render her almost totally powerless to give birth on her own?

And how about experiencing sexual orgasm "by the clock" as well? Would you want some guy standing next to you with a clock at a most supreme moment of sexual bliss telling you that it was all wrong if it wasn't "on time?" Well, what's the difference? How well would you have a full and satisfying experience of any sexual interaction if *every single person* was supposed to do so in *exactly* the same amount of time, in every single circumstance? Your sexual energy would die pretty fast, wouldn't it? So too, does the energy of birth with a gigantic clock sitting on top of it. Then you really *do* have an emergency and the whole thing becomes a self-fulfilling prophecy. Why does this happen? Because the clock is designed to control nature and all of our physical interactions with it. Under the suppression of that control, many things die in our experience.

Have you ever felt yourself to be a "prisoner" of time? How ironic that the clock is, in truth, a gigantic, planetary jail cell.

Let's talk now about calendars. Calendars represent the way in which we measure the *orbit* of our planet earth around our sun. Take a look at the next two diagrams, Diagrams B and C.

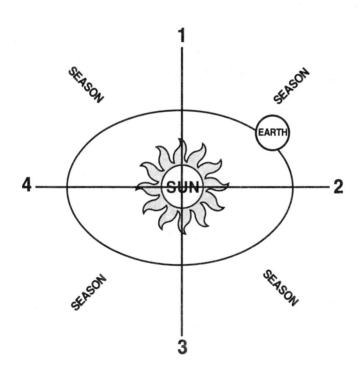

Diagram B

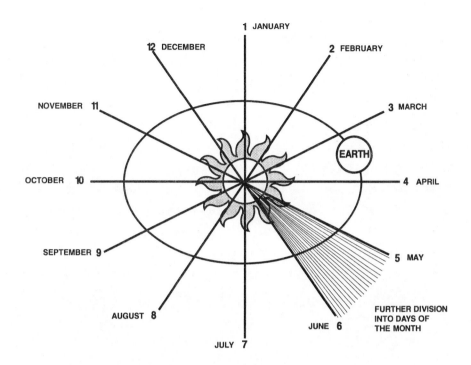

Diagram C

In these two diagrams, we slice the earth's orbit up as though it were some kind of a pie. First, we slice it in fours and label each quadrant a "season." It is remarkable how the *real* seasons in Nature simply do not correspond to the artificial calendar of seasons. Does the "first day of winter," the "first day of summer," the "first day of spring," or the "first day of fall" ever *really* feel like the first day of that season? No, almost never. That concept is so utterly disconnected from the truth of nature's graceful flow of seasons, which is unmarked by lines of any kind. To say that any season starts on the same, exact day of every single year, is about as ludicrous as saying that night starts at exactly the same second, every single day. Yet we believe that it does! 6:00 p.m., right? Everyday at 6:00 p.m., so-called "night" begins. In the summertime, everybody marvels because "it's still light" at 6:00 p.m.! Amazing!

Next, we divide each of these four quadrants into thirds, to obtain a total of 12 calendar months. Now, we have a pie cut into 12 sections. And as if that wasn't enough, each of these pie pieces has to be cut up even further, and we figure out how many times the earth rotates through 24 bars of the clock during the course of each month, and then divide that month into that many sections. The problem is, of course, that 365 days is not really divisible by 12, and you have some messy, extra days sticking out and nowhere to put them, so you just add them on randomly at the end of certain months, subtract another one from another month, and hope the heck that no one notices! Have you ever wondered why we don't have 13 months? 365 days is neatly divisible by 13, and lo and behold, it actually corresponds to the cycle of the moon, at 28 days per month! But, gosh, you know, that's just too powerful and *definitely* too close to nature. Better to slip by as really poor mathematicians, and make sure that we stay *totally* out of sync with our planet by using a 12 month calendar. Yet, this totally out-of-sync, mathematically poor calendar is completely deliberate. You can't believe that our scientists are that dumb as to have miscalculated things this much! So why did they do it? Well, let's just say that it was more important to have it divisible by 4, than anything else. And if the earth and its orbital rotational cycles won't fit, then that's just too darn bad. We'll *make* it fit, by god! Some things are just more important than others.

And don't forget the extra day that's *still* sticking out, even after all this tinkering, which has to be added on to February every four years. It's called "leap year" because it's when you blatantly leap over the truth yet another time and pretend it doesn't exist.

So let's talk now about the purpose of this weak, badly constructed, blazing example of poor math that we fondly refer to as our calendar. To base your existence on the calendar is like living in a house perched on a hill at the edge of a cliff, the foundation of which is being held together by matchsticks and twigs. Your chances of feeling secure are next to none, because you haven't got a prayer of feeling that your life exists in union with the Universe or anything else real, for that matter.

In the twelve-month calendar, your life exists in a void, completely disconnected from reality, where you must now be told, by the calendar itself, when to do what in this artificial illusion.

Think of it this way. At the moment of your birth (which is *never* accurately recorded anyway, how can it be?) the clock starts ticking. From that moment on, you will be measured, judged, evaluated, and told *precisely* what to do and when, for the rest of your life, all based upon where you stand in relationship to that measuring device. To show how powerfully influential artificial time is in our world, the human species is the *only* species on the planet that uses a clock to determine the *moment* of our birth and the *moment* of our death. It's almost as though without that calendar date and clock minute, we don't really *know* if someone was actually born or really even died! What do you think a birth certificate and certificate of death are all about? They certify that the almighty clock has cut you off from reality at the beginning of your life and cut you off again at the end. The clock, dear friends, is what marks our entry into the illusion produced by the void which our space travelers have noted around our planet. It also marks our so-called departure from that void at the end. You see, we must have these moments marked because it gives us the illusion of greater control.

Do you doubt that there's a void in our experience? Then why indeed do we need these clocks and calendars to tell us what to do, where we should be, and to measure our progress accordingly? People determine their entire sense of self worth based on how they experience themselves in relationship to the clock. Fortunately for us, the animals, insects, birds, plants, fishes, and other creatures of the earth don't have or recognize the existence of clocks and calendars, and don't carry watches either. If they did, we'd be in *big* trouble figuring out how to negotiate and control all of them in relationship to our clocks.

So why are we bringing all of this up? The reason is that the first question people usually have when they begin to recognize that there is indeed a problem on planet earth, which we are calling the source of fear, is *when* did it happen and *how* did it begin? The key word in this question is *when*. What they mean is on what precise *date* did it occur and how many millenniums ago? They want to know this because they figure that if they know when, then they can go back historically and measure what was happening before that moment, measure again what was happening after that moment, subtract the difference and lo and behold, find the "how" of it all and therefore the cure!

This mathematical approach will not work, you see, because the source of fear itself is what is producing our distorted perspective on time, measuring, and mathematics in the first place! It would be like looking through the eyes of the beast to find the cure. It won't happen!

So to find the key to the final elimination of the source of fear, we must center ourselves and orient our approach in a no-time place. This, dear friends, is the place of unlimited power and this is precisely what our space travelers are going to do. From here, you can see *everything*!

Chapter 7

The Absence

At last, we have arrived! Our wondrous space crew has found the coordinates they were looking for in the Universal Arc of Timelessness. From their powerful vantage point in the eternal Now they are preparing the ship's sensors to make contact with earth's dimension of reality and positioning their ship in such a way as to be able to receive the information that they are seeking.

The captain calls all of his highest officers into a special viewing room, where they will interact with the ship's computer in such a way as to gain full access to whatever it is they need to know. The computer will now provide them with all of that information, as everyone sits back and prepares to find out what is really happening on planet earth.

The captain dims the lights and everyone takes their seats as a brightly lit screen appears before them. The computer will now translate the information being received by the ship's sensors into a language that they can understand.

The amazing thing about this brilliant ship is that it possesses the capability of translating any sort of information, from any connecting world, into a language that the observer is able to understand.

Let us imagine that we, too, are receiving the same information in our language, as well.

We begin with an imaginary story about a fictitious character to illustrate a fascinating point. Our language is not equipped to provide us with a way to describe the origin of certain things, so the computer instead will create a story for us to illustrate that point.

Once upon a time there was a strange little creature who lived in the Universe and spent all of its time romping and playing among the stars. One day, the little creature found that it was feeling bored and sat back to observe the heavens and how creation was made. It started to wonder about things. The little creature noticed that everything in the Universe existed as a statement of "I am" something. Everything was a statement, ultimately, of "I am Omnipresence" in individual form. It started to wonder about the fact that everything in life was so radiantly present. It wondered and it wondered and it thought and thought, and eventually it thought so hard about the same thing, that it accidentally bumped into its own mind! That bump produced a jar in its consciousness and suddenly the little creature began to wonder even more. "Hmmm," it thought to itself, "I wonder. Everything in the Universe is a manifesting statement of Presence. Everything in the Universe is manifesting as 'I *am*' something. Everything is a statement of what it *is*." The little creature thought again. "I wonder," it said, "I wonder if it is possible for something to be known by what it *isn't* rather than by what it is?"

With that, the little creature clapped its hands together in glee. "Oh, how exciting. What fun! I wonder if I might create such a thing?" And with that, the funny little creature began turning somersaults, thinking of how humorous it would be to see something bouncing all over the Universe trying to be what it's *not*.

"But how might I create such a thing?" the little creature sat down and thought to itself. "It would be very difficult to create something that exists as what it isn't in a Universe where everything exists as what it *is*! Oh my, I don't know if it's possible," thought the little creature sadly, and it put its head in its hands and looked more bored than ever before, as it contemplated a whole Universe of Omnipresent Oneness.

Then, suddenly, the funny creature had an idea! "I know! I'll just *say* that this thing *isn't* something, even though it *is*! Eureka!" The funny little creature then began jumping and dancing and romping all over the place, thinking of how funny this "I am *not*" would look bouncing around in the Universe.

Now, dear friends, what do you suppose you would have to do in order to create "I am *not*" in an infinite Universe where *everything* exists as a statement of "I am" Omnipresence? It sounds impossible, right? Well, in truth it is impossible. There is no way for anything to exist as what it is *not*, in a Universe of I *am* infinitely present, *everywhere*. So what do you do?

Well, what the fictitious character in our little story just did, was to invent the first, original *lie*.

You see, the only way to create "I am *not*" in an Omnipresent Universe is to lie about it, because it will never be the truth. Picture infinity. It is everywhere, all at once. There is *no* place that is *not* infinite, because if there were, then infinity would not exist. You can't have "some" infinity over here in this place and no infinity over there in that place. So how does this lie of "I am not" get created? Well, all that you need to understand is that a lie exists in resistance to the truth. You have the truth, which is "I am" and that truth exists everywhere and can't be changed. Period. So the only way to create this little thing that our creature was talking about is to generate a *resistance* to that truth.

Let us now watch as the ship's computer gives us all of the information about the source of this strange, alien energy that is wreaking such tremendous havoc on our planet earth.

We will begin with Diagram A on the next page.

Diagram A represents a blank screen of Omnipresence. On

this screen, we will witness infinity. The screen is infinite in all directions. It has no boundaries or borders. In this infinite space resides Omnipresence, the power and love that creates and manifests all things.

We will now follow with Diagram B on the opposite page.

This drawing illustrates how life comes into being in this powerful field of Omnipresent energy. Each point represents

Diagram A

some aspect of creation as it exists in a radiating flow of energy, expansion, and evolution.

Let us move now to Diagram C on the next page.

In Diagram C, we see how each aspect of creation is manifesting as a statement of "*I am*" Omnipresence. Every element in creation thus *contributes* itself and its infinite presence in a radiating flow of energy to the surrounding Universe. All

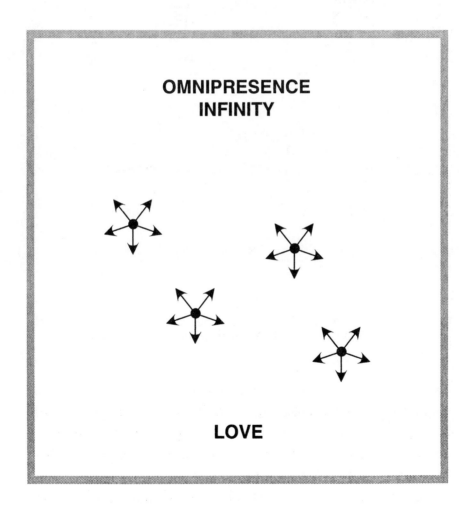

Diagram B

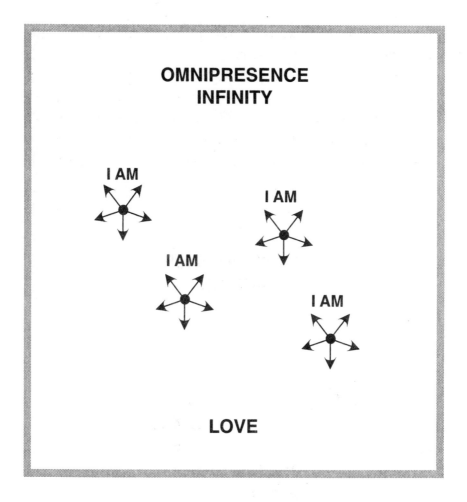

Diagram C

things exist in contribution in a radiating flow.

Now we move to Diagram D on the opposite page. We will now observe the basic nature of this strange phenomenon in space and how it is constructed as a basic principle which is wreaking all of the havoc on planet earth.

Diagram D shows the *first* element of this phenomenon, which is *resistance*. The "X" represents the point at which the

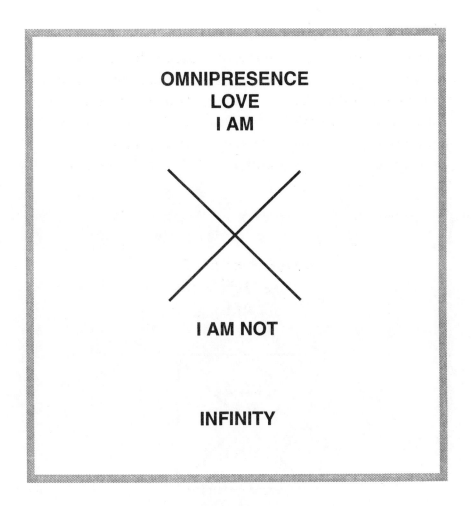

Diagram D

resistance begins. This resistance point has no size, as you cannot resist a "part" of infinity. You either resist all of it, or none of it. So for the sake of discussion, let's say that it could be minute and tiny and still inflict the same amount of destruction.

The "X" is the symbol for "I am *not*." It is a resistance factor and that is all. The "X" is there to resist the truth of Omnipresence.

Now let us move to Diagram E.

This illustration is very interesting, because the moment the resistance or the "X" establishes itself, an instantaneous wall appears around it to mark the space within which this phenomenon resists Omnipresence. This space also simultaneously marks the space within which the phenomenon exists. The space immediately becomes finite. Any and all experience of

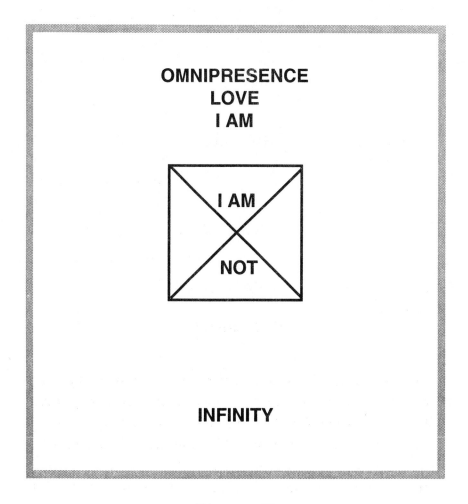

Diagram E

infinity instantly disappears. This phenomenon has now established itself in the Universe as a "law" or principle, that by nature of design alone, produces the most destructive flow of energy ever conceived in the cosmos.

Let us witness now, how that works. We will start with a simple illustration of a common vacuum to use as a model for us to understand some of the underlying principles upon which this phenomenon is based.

In Diagram F at the bottom of this page, we see a circle which represents a sphere. This sphere exists in an environment of air, yet within the sphere there is *no* air. The walls of the sphere exist to *resist* the air and keep it out of that finite space within. So inside the sphere, we have a vacuum or a void. Basically a condition of *no* air.

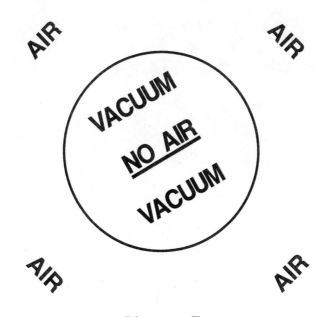

Diagram F

We will now show you how a reverse-flow of energy is sourced. Let's look at the next diagram, which is Diagram G, below.

What is happening in this picture? The air is pressing against the walls of the vacuum. The degree to which the walls *resist* the entry of air into that space, equals exactly the degree of pressure that the air exerts upon those walls. Now what happens if we are to poke a tiny hole in the wall of the vacuum? Look at the next illustration to find out.

If you poke a hole in the side of the vacuum, as in Diagram H on the opposite page, what happens is that the air rushes in with incredible force. The vacuum will produce *suction* as that voided space draws the air into itself. If we were to talk about that suction in human terms, we could say that it equates *need*. Now here is the ultimate paradox that exists within the

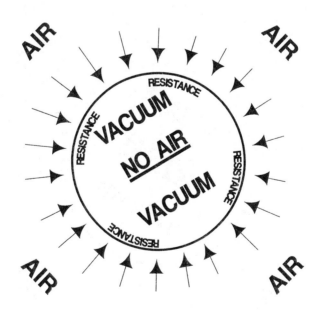

Diagram G

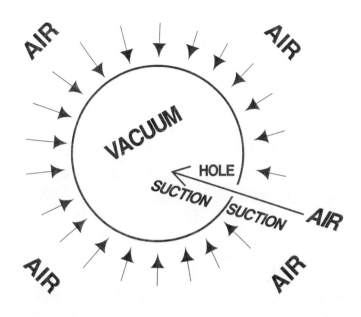

Diagram H

vacuum. The vacuum itself resists the air and must *maintain that resistance* in order to survive. The moment the air enters into that space, the vacuum will cease to exist. So in that way of viewing it, the air constitutes a *threat* to the survival of the vacuum. Yet, the vacuum itself needs the air! The degree of need will be exactly proportional to the degree of resistance. You can see the need manifesting through the degree of suction that the vacuum has the potential to produce. A vacuum has only one purpose to its existence and that is survival. It cannot contribute anything and can only *take* from the surrounding environment. In this case, the surrounding environment is air, and the vacuum can do only one of two things. It either *resists* the air, or it *takes* the air into itself. Picture a spherical vacuum: Now imagine poking holes in it all around its walls, which are intended to resist the air. Can you see the energy? The existence of the vacuum causes intense suction to occur immediately into its center. The suction manifests in a reverse-flow, which is the opposite of contribution.

Now let's observe how the alien phenomenon that we have been observing follows these exact same principles of a vacuum in terms of how it is designed. Have you figured out already why it is termed "alien?" That's right. It's because it exists in resistance to life (Omnipresence) and is *against* life, therefore it is alien to life, or put another way, anti-life. Simple, isn't it? Now let's see why "life" or Omnipresence is a threat to this phenomenon.

Look at the next diagram, which is Diagram I, on the opposite page.

Like the vacuum being "threatened" by air, this alien phenomenon is equally threatened by Omnipresence, because that is the thing it is resisting. A vacuum, however, is a finite example and in the case of an air-filled environment, there is a limit as to how much pressure the surrounding environment of air can exert upon the vacuum itself. Yet even with the smallest ratio of air to "no air" the force of suction can still be extremely powerful. How about the pressurized cabin in an aircraft flying at 24,000 feet? In this case, there is more air (air pressure) inside the cabin and less air (air pressure) outside. If you break a hole in the window of this plane, everything inside will be sucked out with an incredible force. And this ratio is minute compared to the situation with this phenomenon.

As you see in the picture, the "I am not" is resisting Omnipresence. It is actually resisting infinity. What sort of a ratio or difference is there between infinity and "*not*" infinity? Can you imagine the potential for suction and reverse-flow in this case? The suction potential is infinite, because the resistance is to

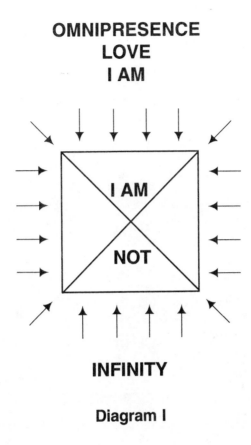

OMNIPRESENCE
LOVE
I AM

INFINITY

Diagram I

infinity. What this means is that the "need," which is the suction potential, can never be filled. It can never be satisfied. In a manner of speaking, what you now have is a principle that manifests as a "voracious beast" meaning that its need is endless and its potential for reverse-flow is equally as unlimited.

So what happens when a force as destructive as this is unleashed into the Universe? Let's continue on and find out.

Let's now observe two more diagrams.

In Diagram J, on page 96, everything is an expression of infinity manifesting in a radiating flow. Now look at Diagram K on page 97.

OMNIPRESENCE

INFINITY

THE UNIVERSE

I AM

LOVE

Diagram J

In Diagram K, the resistance of "I am *not*" creates the illusion of finite space, because now there is the illusion of two opposing-things (the space inside the box and the space outside the box), neither of which can be infinite. From this perspective, not only does the box appear finite, but the whole Universe does as well. Remember finite and infinite cannot coexist in the same reality. Infinity is either everything, or it doesn't exist at all, in which case everything becomes finite. Even Omnipresence appears finite and is now mistaken as "God," a finite identity which creates everything else and is perceived to exist in separation from that creation. As you can see, it does not take very long before there are more and more

THE UNIVERSE ← FINITE

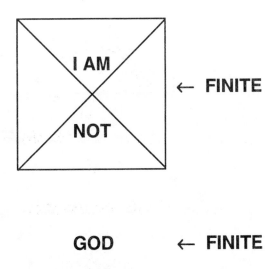

GOD ← FINITE

Diagram K

elements existing in separation from one another. Which leads us to the next amazing aspect of this phenomenon, which causes it to be even more destructive.

In the Universe, there exists true magnetism which is the basis upon which all of creation connects with itself and produces interaction, harmony, and the experience of oneness and integration with every individual aspect of itself. This alien phenomenon cannot simply exist in a void, in perpetual "need" of Omnipresence, for if that were the case, Omnipresence would immediately enter that voided space and the phenomenon would cease to exist. So this phenomenon had to have a way to engage with creation in such a way as to create the

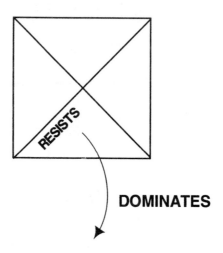

THE UNIVERSE

Diagram L

illusion of it being fulfilled, without actually being fulfilled in truth—which would immediately cause it to become extinct. The only way to engage with creation is via some magnetic property and through what we have described so far, the perfect reversal of real magnetism is actually inherent in the design of this phenomenon. We will call this reverse-flow magnetism "dominate/be dominated." Here's how it works. Let's look at the next two diagrams.

In Diagram L, on this page, we can see where this phenomenon is *dominating* the entire Universe through its act of resistance to Omnipresence.

In Diagram M, on the opposite page, we see that the phenomenon is also *being dominated* by the Universe, because like the air to the vacuum, the Universe (being a manifestation of Omnipres-

THE UNIVERSE

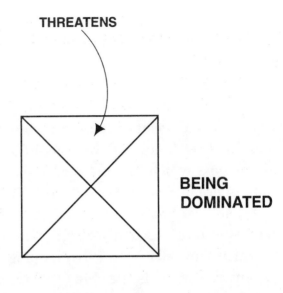

Diagram M

ence) simultaneously threatens the existence of the void.

What this then produces along the "wall" of this phenomenon (which we will now refer to as the Absence) is an alternating frequency of energy called dominate/be dominated. In other words, the absence is dominating and being dominated all at the same time. Likewise, the finite Universe with which it interacts is *also* dominating and being dominated at the very same time. This creates a magnetic "locking on" effect, which makes it almost impossible to "shake this thing off" once it's got you. Its power to lock on within any given reality is so pervasive that it becomes impossible to experience reality once it's there, which is why our space travelers were so exceedingly cautious about their approach. This phenomenon will turn everything around 180 degrees and the next thing you know, you'll be saying the *illusion* is reality and reality is an illusion.

Let us now observe this absence with all of its fundamental principles intact. Please observe the diagram on the opposite page, Diagram N.

In this diagram you can see the origin of this phenomenon through the element of resistance to Omnipresence, represented by the "X," a statement of "I am *not*" which is the original lie or illusion. This "I am *not*" produces the illusion of a finite space, or box, which literally manifests as an "absence" of Omnipresence in that space. Although this is yet another illusion, it is still very powerful, nonetheless, and produces a tremendous need or "suction" energy as represented by the arrows which show all of the energy moving in reverse. Because this phenomenon exists as a void or an absence, it only has the potential to *take* from the surrounding environment, and can contribute nothing, because it *is* nothing. Next, the duality set up by its existence produces the illusion that everything is finite and therefore exists in opposition to one another. This opposing factor generates a reverse-magnetic principle of dominate/be dominated which is indicated by the alternating wave lines, " ((((((", around the edges of the box .

Now you can see this phenomenon fully intact and prepared to move into whatever reality it can, and basically *take* from that reality, deplete it, and then move on to the next one. (Does this sound familiar in terms of our collective behavior on planet earth?)

We call this phenomenon the Absence, or to put it more accurately in human terms, the source of fear. Why? Because *fear* is what it feels like to experience this void. It is the missing experience of Omnipresence. The *energy* of fear is found in the alternating frequency of dominate/be dominated, which is

THE ABSENCE

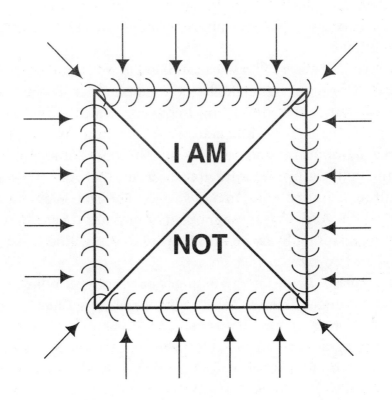

I AM

NOT

THE SOURCE OF FEAR

Diagram N

what produces the wall around the absence itself. As long as dominate/be dominated can be sustained, then there is not a "chance in Hell," as they say, that Omnipresence will ever enter into that space and fill it with love. The problem is that the answer is not as simple as just "letting go," because the principle itself will actually *prevent* you from doing that. This is why the only answer is to permanently eliminate that phenomenon.

Let us now observe how fear and anger are intimately tied together through dominate/be dominated. This absence always produces this alternating frequency, which produces a reverse-flow magnetic. Magnetism refers to the attraction produced by opposite poles of energy. Through dominate/be dominated, things are attracted to each other out of *need*, resulting from the void, in a desire to take from each other and fill the void. In *true* magnetism, things are attracted out of love, resulting from a natural desire to contribute to each other and co-create.

"Dominate" is the energy of anger or resistance. Wherever there is a threat, there will be anger, which is an attempt to *resist* the threat. Yet simultaneously, the threat produces a feeling of being dominated, which is the energy of fear. So "dominate" and "be dominated" will always be attracted to each other like two irreversible magnets. Where there is anger, you will always find fear. This is why victim and abuser always seem to be magnetically "attached" to one another in ways that make it seem impossible to separate in spite of their best interests. People are often confused as to why, in dysfunctional relationships, victims will stay with abusers and abusers (who exhibit so much disdain for their victims) will stay with their victims. Wouldn't you think they would both just leave each other immediately and want nothing to do with each other any longer?

How come they don't? On the surface, the abuser dominates the victim in anger and in rage. Yet, they are also being completely dominated by the victim because they exhibit absolutely no control of their actions when they are around that person. Thus their abusive actions will produce an underlying fear in themselves at their total *lack* of control, because they are really feeling dominated, which only makes them angrier at their victim (more threatened) and the cycle starts all over again. The victim's surface experience is clearly one of fear, or being threatened and totally dominated. Yet a victim's fear will always be followed by rage and anger, which for them will be their underlying experience.

Let's look at Diagram O below to understand this more clearly.

* OPPOSITE POLES OF ENERGY *

DOMINATE / BE DOMINATED
(Anger) / (Fear)

REVERSE-FLOW MAGNETIC

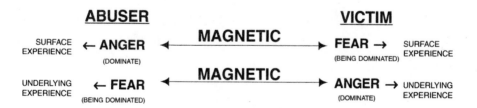

ABUSER		VICTIM
SURFACE EXPERIENCE ← ANGER (DOMINATE)	**MAGNETIC** ⟶	FEAR → (BEING DOMINATED) SURFACE EXPERIENCE
UNDERLYING EXPERIENCE ← FEAR (BEING DOMINATED)	**MAGNETIC** ⟶	ANGER → (DOMINATE) UNDERLYING EXPERIENCE

**DRAWN TO BE TOGETHER
OUT OF *NEED***

Diagram O

This illustration shows the underlying magnetic principle which holds victim and abuser together. In this diagram we see how victim and abuser magnetically "plug in" to each other via these opposing poles of reverse-flow energy. This explains the confusing attachment that they often exhibit for each other, even though it is destructive to both parties. Their relationship exhibits every single characteristic of the principle known as "the source of fear."

This explains why people on earth are so often confused by their own dysfunctional behavior, when they perceive that behavior to be a product of who they really are. Knowing that the strange and often destructive behavior that we witness within ourselves and among ourselves on this beautiful planet earth is the result of a scientific, reverse-flow *principle*, rather than an expression of who we are can change *everything*.

This simple principle, known as "the source of fear," is basically what's causing all of the trouble here on our planet.

Chapter 8

The Body, Mind, and Emotions

The next question, of course, is how did this phenomenon known as "the source of fear" enter our planetary dimension of earth, and what is it doing here?

As our space travelers observed earlier, the source of fear has entered our dimension of reality via the space/time continuum of planet earth. This phenomenon enters into a reality via the basic laws and principles of magnetics. It could not enter in based upon pure need alone, because there would be no way for it to engage. The question, "What is it doing here?" can best be answered by looking at the pure motive of existence that this phenomenon carries within itself, which is based solely upon its design.

First of all, let us say that there is no such thing, in reality, as anything which is inherently "evil" because by now you might be thinking, "Boy oh boy, if this thing has the power to cause so much destruction and suffering on our planet, then it must be *really* evil!" Believe it or not, the very concept of "good and evil" is actually a product of this phenomenon, itself. It is a polarized concept which implies, once again, that good and so-called evil are both natural, inherent parts of Reality existing at odds with one another and that we should strive to overcome the evil in favor of the good. This is basically a trick, you see, because if you can convince yourself that this battle is the "game" of life, then you will never, ever win, for that evil will always come back to haunt you no matter how "good" you become. It will always exist as a shadow in your mind and eventually you will begin to wonder, "If I'm so *good*, then how come I still have no experience of Omnipresence???"

It's almost as though there's this underlying invisible "finger" that keeps pointing us away from the *real* story of what's actually going on here and getting us all caught up in the game of dominate/be dominated. You know, *dominate* the evil with the good (meaning to overcome it), or in some instances dominate the good with the evil, instead. Either way, the person who's doing the dominating always thinks he or she is right, right? Because their side is good and the other guy's side is *always* just, plain wrong. How do you think it is that religions have found it so necessary, on many occasions, to *kill* people for the sake of their belief? Well, in their minds they were simply trying to dominate those person's wrong beliefs, by getting rid of the believers and therefore establishing, so they thought, only *good* beliefs and *right* beliefs in the world. The real problem comes in, of course, when you have different religions with conflicting beliefs all trying to coexist in the same world. Then you have *war*, right? One side trying to dominate the other. The side who wins is the *right* side. You see, in the scenario of dominate/be dominated, life is completely and utterly irrelevant. The only thing that matters is who wins the battle, because it's always a battle of right versus wrong. The funny thing is, of course, that everyone participating in the battle believes that *they*, of course, are *right*. So what you have is a whole bunch of people thinking that they are right and that everyone else is wrong. No wonder there's so much fighting going on, on our planet!

So this alien phenomenon enters into our dimension of space/time reality through a magnetic interface with that dimension, via the absence's reverse-flow field of magnetism, the frequency of dominate/be dominated, which is the frequency of fear itself. For what purpose? For the purpose of creating illusions to fulfill its voracious need. Remember that at "the heart of the beast," so to speak, you will find only a void. A total absence of the experience of Omnipresence, which is an *illusion* based upon the original lie of "I am *not*" and its accompanying resistance to the truth.

That void produces a powerful, infinite need that exactly corresponds to the infinite power that is being resisted within that space. Now here's the tricky part. The absence exists in total survival, just like the vacuum, and can never have that need fulfilled or it will cease to exist altogether. Its only purpose is to survive, yet the need is ever-pressing. So we now have two conflicting energies, just like the vacuum, where there is a tremendous *need* for fulfillment and a simultaneous, equal level of *resistance* to that fulfillment. What would you call the balance of these two opposing forces in human terms? Frustration, of course! Frustration is most definitely an extremely painful experience because it always exists as a combination of need and resistance to the fulfillment of that need. There is an energy behind frustration that calls out for that need to be met, even though it can only be met under the condition that the resistance stays in place, because the survival of the entity is at stake. And survival will always take the highest priority in this strange world of illusion produced by the Absence. So how do you meet the need and yet keep the resistance firmly in place? Sounds impossible, doesn't it? Not if you, as a human being, *believe* that you are the void. In the case of the void, of course, that's exactly what it is, a void. So the void wants the need fulfilled, but doesn't want to disappear in the process. After all, what fun is it having a need fulfilled if you aren't going to be there to appreciate it? This is a silly way of saying it, but it makes the point. Understand, however, that there exists *no feeling* in this Absence. It is a void and is only acting based on nature of its design alone. Period. It exists almost as a machine, unable to think and feel, and possessing no life force of any kind, whatsoever. It is the energy of death, in the true sense of the word. Some of you might be feeling "sorry" for this poor phenomenon, being so "frustrated" and all. Some do-gooder types might actually get the brilliant idea of trying to "help" it. You know, talk to it or reason with it in some way. It is impossible to reason with a void whose sole purpose is survival of itself and whose survival can only be insured to the extent that it continues to behave in all of the ways that *you* think you'd like to change.

So how does this phenomenon achieve the fascinating feat of appearing to have its need met, without actually doing so? The answer to that question begins with the fact that this absence cannot just exist out in the Universe as a void, all by itself, because it would instantly cease to exist as a viable principle. The power of Omnipresence would fill that space or that illusion almost instantly. It must therefore find some way in which to "attach" itself to something real, our dimension of reality for example, and then proceed to induce that reality to act in accordance with its own design. What this does is to create a physical manifestation of dominate/be dominated, which is the magnetic energy that comprises the "wall" of this absence that is designed to keep Omnipresence out and the void intact.

Now, you might ask, "Well, how come this thing doesn't just make its *own* wall? Why does it have to involve us or anything else for that matter?" Try to remember that this phenomenon exists only as an energetic *principle*. It is not a thing which contains any substance. It is completely illusionary and cannot exist in a Universe where everything is real, unless it can somehow interface with a particular reality and "act out its principles" through the thing that is real. This is literally the only way in which it can continue to survive indefinitely.

The Absence itself "feeds" off of our illusions which are ultimately generated by itself. So the dominate/be dominated scenario which it enacts through our consciousness is the way in which it continues to survive, while feeding off of all of our unmet needs and illusions, which are created only by itself.

Let us now examine how this phenomenon, termed the source of fear, exists within our consciousness and affects literally everything that we do. Let us begin where all things begin, with a discussion of Omnipresence. Omnipresence manifests itself through us via what we will call our powerful, human presence. Never underestimate the power of that presence in human form, because it is literally an expression of God itself. This presence is who we are and exists as an individual manifestation of Omnipresence. Our human presence, which is infinite, manifests itself on this planet via our wonderful human bodies, which are specifically designed to conduct the energy of that presence in a radiating flow of love.

So where do we first feel that experience of our true self, which is this infinite human presence and where does it enter into our physical experience upon this beautiful planet earth? The answer is through our hearts, that place within us through which we are connected to the entire Universe. Never underestimate the power of that human presence to manifest through us and contribute something of great power, love, and beauty upon this planet earth. It is exactly what we are designed for. We are designed to conduct the full magnitude, energy, and presence of our human selves upon this earth in a radiating flow of love, which we will first experience in our hearts as a powerful feeling of love and divine presence. This presence immediately fulfills us and then moves on to express itself

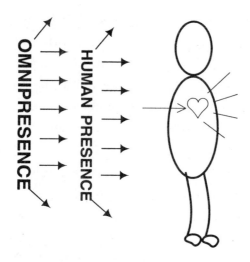

Diagram A

outwardly in a contributing flow of energy. Let's observe some diagrams that will show us how this works.

In Diagram A, on this page, we see how Omnipresence is manifesting itself as human presence in the radiating flow of creation. That experience of infinite, radiating love first enters our physical experience here on earth, via our hearts, as a powerful emotion or feeling.

From here, that experience must continue to flow through our system in such a way as to ultimately express itself in outward contribution. This is where it ultimately makes itself known on our planet in a way that it can be recognized and benefit others. But that pure feeling of infinite, Omnipresent energy must somehow be translated in a way that has physical meaning on our particular planetary sphere. So how is this accomplished?

Upon entering our hearts, the power of that energy immediately radiates into our minds or brain. Our mind is filled with light and the impulse of that power stimulates the mind into

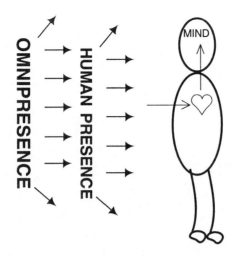

Diagram B

an infinite sense of knowing which allows it to translate that experience into something meaningful within our planetary, earth experience. This does not require any particular effort or "thinking" on the part of our mind. It is automatic and already built in as a natural function of our brilliant selves.

Let us now observe Diagram B, above.

In this drawing, we see the continuation of that radiating flow of energy, which begins with Omnipresence, and continues to manifest as our powerful human presence. It then enters into our earth experience as an impulse of love and fulfillment within our heart, and from there that same impulse (which in the beginning originated as infinity) enters our minds and is translated into something meaningful that pertains to our existence on this planet. This is achieved in the mind by a higher sense of knowing and the immediate recognition of that light and energy which originates in the infinite Universe of Love. The mind is actually able to accomplish this because it is, in truth, already a part of infinite, universal intelligence and

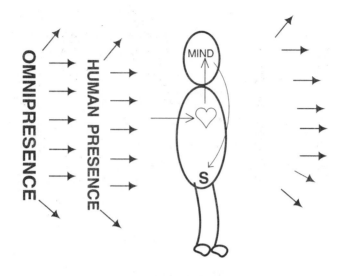

Diagram C

is able to translate that intelligence into an earth-based experience of it in a way that harmonizes with all things.

So now we have gone from *feeling* the energy and love of Omnipresence, through our divine human presence as that impulse first strikes our hearts, to *knowing* the meaning of that experience as it pertains to our experience on this planet as that same impulse moves into and fills our minds with light and infinite presence. Yet feeling and knowing are not enough because this impulse of love must continue to move outward in some form of action or expression which will ultimately allow that presence of the Universe to manifest through us and contribute something upon this earth. Let us now observe the last drawing, Diagram C on this page, to see how this happens.

From the mind, this impulse now travels into the body via our physical, sexual expression of who we are. Now let us clarify for a moment what we mean here by the word sexual. We are not referring to sexual as it is normally used, which is to be limited only to the genitals or "sexual acts" as they are called. We use the word sexual to describe the physical origin of our human bodies and also to describe the fact that we are either man or woman. Our sexual energy has to do with our ability to physically create and therefore it stands to reason that this powerful impulse of love would transmit itself through our minds and into our bodies via our sexual energy of man or woman. From this place it carries with it life force, profound health and physical radiance, and a very magnetic, creative expression of who we really are. As you can see in this last drawing, once this impulse of love and Omnipresence has passed through the entire system of this human being, it can now radiate outward and be felt as *action* manifesting through this individual. The radiating arrows pointing outward show that through this human being we can now recognize God in form, as that Omnipresent energy radiates fully through this person onto the earth.

So the final manifestation of Omnipresence through our human selves after it has passed through our heart in the form of *feeling*, and our mind in the form of *knowing*, is to pass through our physical bodies in the form of *action*. From this incredible alignment of the human form and its innate design to conduct a radiating flow, Omnipresence can manifest and express itself fully and completely through the unlimited divinity of our natural, human selves.

Now what do you suppose happens when the phenomenon known as the source of fear enters into our reality and dramatically affects what happens within our human system?

The point at which the existence of the source of fear can first be felt is in our hearts. The reason for this is because this is the point at which we first connect with Omnipresence in our earth-based experience. Because this absence is based upon a

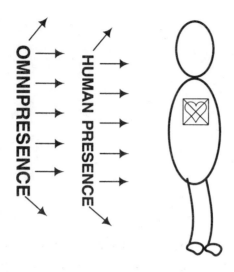

Diagram D

fundamental resistance to Omnipresence, the heart is the place within ourselves where it will first establish its existence, in order to resist that impulse before we ever have a chance to feel it.

Let's look at the next series of drawings which will illustrate what happens when this absence enters our human system.

In Diagram D, above, the absence has established itself in the heart of this human being. This person is no longer able to experience Omnipresence and instead feels only a void or a sense of emptiness that would ultimately be translated into a feeling of "something is missing." This person now feels alone and "cut off" from the Universe. They believe that they must handle everything on their own, because God is no longer an experiential reality in their life and has rather become a concept or a belief. Ultimately this person feels strangely unfulfilled and totally lacking in a powerful experience of who they really are.

Now let's observe the next drawing, which is Diagram E on the opposite page.

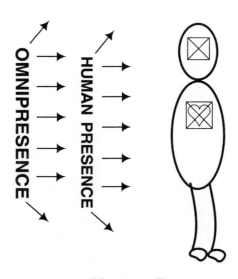

Diagram E

Because there is no experience of Omnipresence in the heart, there is likewise no impulse of that energy in the mind, as well. The mind is therefore "empty" and believes it must function in separation, on its own. It starts to take on an animated version of itself, almost as though it were a separate entity that "talks" to the human bearer of itself. Because it has no infinite impulse of truth flowing into it from the Universe, it has to somehow figure out everything "on its own" by looking outward at physical circumstances and interpreting them in any way that it can. Because the absence sets up an overall reverse-flow of energy within this human being, their mind will tend to interpret life in a reverse-flow as well. Everything in life will now be about survival for this person, rather than about a radiating flow of creation.

Let's now look at Diagram F on the next page.

In this drawing, the physical body receives no true impulse for the empowered, creative action of Omnipresence manifesting in human form. It is weak and is in no way being helped

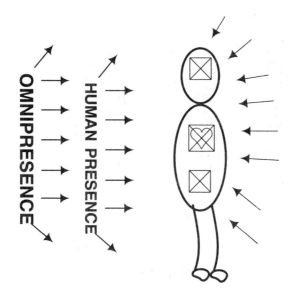

Diagram F

by the mind, which is equally as empty. The best that the mind can do is to artificially bark angry sorts of instructions to the body itself, mostly designed to "protect" it from the perceived threat of life, which is engendered by the ensuing reverse-flow of energy and perception. The dramatically weakened body responds accordingly, for it now has no other purpose except to survive and protect itself at all cost, including the cost of its own creative, self-expression.

Because of the existence of the absence, anything that attempts to move through this person's body in a radiating flow of love and divine self-expression will be interpreted as a threat and reacted to with fear, suspicion, and tremendous self-repression. Have you ever felt that some beautiful way in which you would love to express yourself was met within you with a tremendous fear that it would somehow threaten your survival? Well, this is why. It is important now to realize that with the existence of this absence inside of a person's conscious-ness, their particular form of logic will completely change. There is *real* logic, which is innate and based upon the intelligent truth of Love, Omnipresence, and the interconnectedness of the entire Universe. Then there is a false logic, which doesn't make any sense in terms of the real world of love, that is based on a belief that the only purpose in life is to survive. Which incidentally, in case you hadn't noticed, is the exact same purpose of the Absence itself.

Let us look now at one final drawing, Diagram G, below, which illustrates the difference between a human being in radiating flow and one existing in reverse-flow as a result of the Absence.

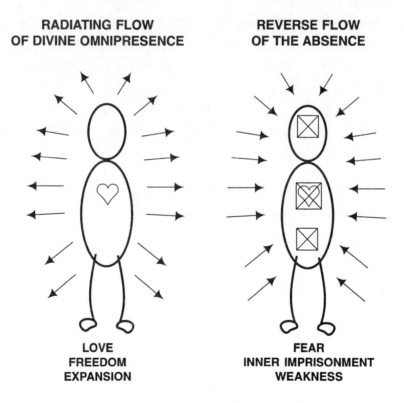

RADIATING FLOW	REVERSE FLOW
OF DIVINE OMNIPRESENCE	OF THE ABSENCE

LOVE	FEAR
FREEDOM	INNER IMPRISONMENT
EXPANSION	WEAKNESS

Diagram G

The first individual is manifesting in a full, radiating expression of who they really are. They are experiencing unlimited freedom and an infinite potential for profound creativity. They are wholly empowered and completely fulfilled within themselves. Their life is for *living* and is about expressing love and contribution. They only express love in all of its many manifestations, because that is the experience that they are constantly being filled with.

The second individual is manifesting what it is like to be "possessed" by the Absence. We use the word possessed because the reverse-flow energy of that phenomenon produces "suction" and need and it is through this effect of energetic suction (like a vacuum) and dominate/be dominated that it literally attaches itself and reverses this person's entire energetic field in such a way that you can't get rid of it. This person is literally being drained of life-force (which we classify as a "normal" everyday experience of being too tired, lethargic, or unmotivated to expand in the powerful expression of who we really are), and exists in a state of total survival. Rather than seeing the world as a powerful arena for self-expression and contribution, this person perceives most of life as a threat and busies themselves with constantly protecting themselves from one perceived threat after another. This they mostly do by taking "no chances" and playing it safe in a routine lifestyle of doing the same thing over and over again so they don't "get hurt."

The person in the first picture is completely free and totally relaxed to be who they truly are. The person in the second picture is totally bound up within themselves, very stressed, and imprisoned by their fear.

It is important here to recognize that *both* drawings represent human beings, each possessing exactly the same characteristics that are being manifested by the first, completely free individual. The only difference between the two is that the second drawing represents our humanity living with the Absence, the source of fear, having infiltrated our human systems and literally creating a prison within our experience which prevents us from being who we really are.

Let us now examine what happens when the Absence, the source of fear, invades an entire planet full of people and causes them to act upon the principles of its own existence. What sort of world will these people create?

Chapter 9

The Artificial Kingdom

In our world, there are many kingdoms of life that can be spoken of with tremendous reverence as each one is a magnificently beautiful manifestation of our beloved earth. These are the kingdoms of Nature. The planetary kingdoms of all of the different life forms that exist on our planet.

And then there is one other kingdom that can hardly be spoken of with reverence and love, for it was designed in complete reversal of Nature itself, is intended to conquer Nature, and will eventually destroy it if allowed to continue in an unbounded way. This kingdom is the artificial kingdom that has been directly produced by human hands.

The artificial world is comprised of anything and everything that goes against Nature and does not integrate with it in any way. If there is any of nature left in its wake, then that natural manifestation is forced to fit in with the artificial. It will never be the other way around. The artificial world will never integrate with Nature, because it can't. It is important to understand here, that *we, too, are Nature*! Due to the influence of the Absence, it is not uncommon for people on earth to perceive themselves as something other than Nature. It's almost as though we believe ourselves to be the "observers" of Nature, rather than a part of it.

Have you ever wondered how it is that human beings can persist in completely destroying the natural environment of this earth—cutting down millions of acres of trees, poisoning everything, killing hundreds of thousands of animals, plants, and creatures of every kind almost to the point of extinction, even destroying each other, as though these actions will have absolutely *no* effect upon our ability to live here? The separation from Nature that is produced by the phenomenon known as the source of fear is the reason why. As we said earlier, you cannot reason with a void or an absence and coincidentally you *also* cannot reason with a human being who is completely possessed by this force. That's why it doesn't matter how much you shout and yell, "Stop! We're killing ourselves and our beautiful planet! Can't you see?" Well, no. They can't see because in the realm of the Absence, *life* is irrelevant, remember? Survival is the only thing that counts. Now here you might say, "Wait a second. But aren't survival and life the same thing?" No. Emphatically no, they are not the same thing. Survival pertains only to a void, while life is the empowered, infinite expression of God itself. The absence "survives" by resisting life, which is Omnipresence. Omnipresence is the *source* of life, which is love. To resist life, as this principle does, means to produce a condition of *no* life, or I am *not* living. Thus we have called it the ultimate force of death. Death, in this case, means the *absence* of life, get it? So survival, in truth, is all about death. It has nothing whatsoever to do with life and living. What does survival mean, after all? It means to *avoid* death, to escape death. This, dear friends, is the entire focus of the source of fear. To resist Omnipresence in order to avoid the extinction of itself. Period. It simply has nothing else going on. Would you like to hear a funny thing about survival? Ultimately, you *never know* if you have indeed survived until the day you die. Because as long as you remain alive, there will always be a question about it. "Will I make it? Will I survive?" Well, survive until when, might we ask? The only point at which you know that, yes, indeed, you have truly accomplished the amazing feat of survival in this life, is when you reach death! Get it? Because then, there's no more need to survive! You've already mastered it. So if death is the only thing that can tell you that you have ultimately survived, then survival is hardly a matter of life. Isn't it true that when a being is in survival death becomes the focal point from which they live and perceive life? Why? Because in survival is the emphasis of trying to avoid death! Which is exactly how the absence manifests.

With survival also comes incredible need, which equates basically with a desperate need to stick around in the current form of one's existence. In human beings it manifests as a need to remain "stuck." To stay the same, as it were, and never change so that in that sameness a person can perceive that they are still around, just the "same" as ever before. The problem with this desperate need for "stuckness" (which is desperate, because it equates survival), is that in that holding pattern of no change, there is also no evolution. This is why we fear change so much. Change is initiated from a place of life and power. Love brings forth incredible change and transformation. Change in human beings is produced by the powerful forces of Nature and Evolution and is ultimately sourced in Omnipresence itself as it continues to express itself in an ever-expanding flow of creation and evolution.

The Absence abhors change and evolution, because evolution is initiated as an act of God or Omnipresence. This, of course, is the ultimate threat and from the perspective of that phenomenon, being stuck in the sense of totally arrested movement and growth, is a clear manifestation of successful resistance to that powerful force of change and evolution.

The artificial kingdom also abhors change. Have you ever noticed that change in our world is always met with incredible resistance? People are afraid of change and will fight it to the bitter end, when change ultimately wins out and things evolve in spite of ourselves.

Let us talk now about this artificial kingdom and describe exactly what it is. The artificial kingdom is comprised of everything in our world that stands out in stark resistance to nature. The most obvious example of this kingdom on a physical level can be found in the huge manifestations of cement buildings and fortresses of concrete cities. The earth will be paved in concrete wherever this kingdom exists. Concrete is a force of resistance. One interesting thing about the nature of concrete, it is not resilient in any way. Things in Nature are resilient; they move, flow, and breathe with change. They can accommodate change and expand with it gracefully.

The artificial world of cities, bricks, and machines cannot expand or accommodate change of any kind. Change, indeed, causes them to break down. Cities and machines are constantly in need of repair due to the effects of the forces of Nature acting upon them. It is fascinating, is it not, that we as humans, under the influence of this Absence, have found ourselves creating building materials that exactly replicate the foundation principles of that phenomenon including the rigidity of its walls and resistance to nature and that which is real? An artificial invention of any kind is said to be "good" to the extent that it can withstand the effects of Nature upon it and remain relatively unchanged. It is said to be of "poor quality" if it tends to break down easily when Nature acts upon it. But this focus is all wrong, you see, because it implies that we are here to do battle with Nature. In this frame of mind, we *take* from Nature, deplete our resources, and twist our usage of those natural resources into something that will eventually destroy Nature, rather than contribute to it.

The influence of this Absence is so pervasive that it actually causes us to extract the natural elements from the earth and somehow alter their very nature in such a way that those same elements which once supported Nature and were a part of it, will now destroy Nature and prevent its growth. Are you unsure of what we're talking about? Well, let's examine things on a vibrational level of existence.

Take a walk out into some natural environment, such as a forest. Bring with you a bag that has a few "artificial" items in it. Some PVC plastic pipe, perhaps, a metal toaster, a can, a glass jar, some aluminum foil, a few broken pieces of concrete, some rubber tires, and last, but not least, a porcelain sink and some plumbing fixtures. Dump all of this "stuff " into a pile next to a tree. (Please do this only in your imagination.) Now, place your hands on the tree. Feel the soil around it. Embrace a large rock sitting next to a stream. Walk through some water and now lay upon the earth. Ahhhh... Can you feel the vibration of life? Now, get up and go over to your "pile." Sit on it, feel it, and touch it. Is it alive? No, of course not. It feels like death, doesn't it? How is that possible? The Absence causes us to use our creative power in a 180 degree absolute reversal of what it truly is. Thus we design weapons, metals, and concrete jungles, all of which hold a vibration that is anti-life and directly corresponds to the same anti-life vibration of the Absence itself.

So artificial, in a sense, means anything that is not *real*. It holds a vibration that is *against* life, rather than a vibration which exists as an expression of life. Now we are not saying that we are against technology and technological advancement. Far from it. True technology is a product of Nature and were we to work in union with Nature, as though we are a part of it (which we *are*, in truth), then we would be so far advanced beyond where we are today that it would make your head spin. As it stands, we can only go so far with our creative capabilities because they are founded in a premise of being *against* Nature. We therefore have nothing to support our creative capabilities and can only *take* from Nature and turn that energy into a reverse-flow. Additionally, we are also stuck with the premise of that Absence, which says that things must remain rigid and unchanged in order to survive. This is always the premise when one's existence is about resisting life in order to survive.

So what is the nature of the artificial kingdom and how do we fit in? The artificial kingdom is based solely on survival. Its only motive is to stay around and remain in existence, no matter what. Because it does not integrate with Nature and *resists* Nature wholeheartedly, it is in constant need of upkeep and must also be artificially sustained by the very human hands that made it. It exists in reverse-flow and rather than contributing to life, earth, and humanity, it *takes* energy from all three. In human terms, this means that our stated purpose for existence in the so-called modern world, is to have a job, make money, and use the energy of that money in order to survive.

Here's how it works. The artificial kingdom exists in a constant state of falling apart within the world of nature, because Nature will inevitably take it back into itself and make it a part of the earth once again (a good reason to get rid of Nature, right? Maybe that explains cutting down all those trees!) The artificial kingdom therefore needs something equally as artificial, because it can't trust Nature (Nature is the enemy to its survival, right?) to hold it together and keep it running smoothly, and therefore "alive." Staying alive ultimately means that it continues to survive in *spite* of Nature, not because of it.

Humans are the obvious choice for this artificial energy of support and sustenance, because humans are the ones who ultimately *made* the artificial kingdom in the first place. Because the artificial kingdom was created out of a reverse-flow energy of need, resistance, and survival, it demands exactly the same reverse-flow patterning in the humans who interact with it. In order to integrate with the artificial world, one must basically interact with it in a reverse-flow way.

Let's start with the purpose of human life. In the *real* world (which is not the artificial, as so many people are fond of believing) the purpose of human life is to exist as a contributing, creative force of evolution and expansion. The motivation to enact this purpose is love and an appreciation of life. The Universe is completely behind this powerful human manifestation of radiating flow and this flow, as well, exists as a direct expression of Omnipresence itself. Ultimately there is unlimited power, fulfillment, and unimpeded, creative self-expression in that flow of energy. This is the existence of humanity in the real world.

In the artificial world, the purpose for human life changes altogether. The ultimate purpose in the "fake" world (one that is based upon illusion and that which is *not* real) is one thing and one thing only. Survival. So a human being's intended purpose here is to "survive" the experience of being alive and existing on this planet. The artificial kingdom also exists solely to survive because, like the Absence, it cannot contribute anything to the natural world.

So the artificial kingdom looks at people and people look at the artificial kingdom. Both are equally based in survival. So they say to one another, "Let's make a deal." The artificial kingdom says to the humans, "You take care of me, keep me running, and keep me alive to further deplete the earth and all its resources (including you, by the way) so that I can fulfill the voracious need of the 'thing' which is ultimately behind my entire existence, and in return for that, I will keep you surviving as well, by giving you *only enough money* on which to survive." Well, it makes sense, doesn't it? In a world where the only purpose is to survive, that's all you *need*, right? Enough money to "live on." Why do you think everyone's wages are so low?

So the people, who are *very* much afraid because in their experience of this Absence, there is no Universe, no God, no Love (and don't think that philosophical "beliefs" that these are real will be adequate, because they won't) to support them, take care of them, and manifest through them, believe that they are entirely on their own, living in a void (which they are), and by gosh, this deal sounds pretty good to them! So in their mutual need created by living in the void produced by this Absence, the people and the artificial kingdom agree to work together and help each other survive, since nothing else in the Universe is there to accomplish that feat. It will be called "having a job." They figure that "job" is a good word for it, because it will be difficult, arduous, and painful to do. Why? Because a person will have to go against every natural instinct of freedom and creative self-expression in order to do it.

So how does this job thing work? Well, it's simple. The people approach it in a reverse-flow of survival and the company (which represents the artificial kingdom) also approaches it in the same reverse-flow of need and greed. Both are needy and equally greedy. Their agreement is to "take" something from each other and call it a fair trade. The company says, "I want to *take* from you your time, your energy, and your ability to create. In exchange for my taking from you, you get to take something from me. Money. But only enough for survival, because that's all you need, right? But I don't require that much from you either. A low-quality version of forcing yourself to do something that you hate, that is completely against your will, will be just fine for me." So each depletes the other. The company greedily takes as much time and energy away from the employee "slaves" as it can, while the employee slaves are equally as greedy about doing as little as possible for the most amount of money. In their mutual need/greed scenario of dominate/be dominated they become angry and start to bad mouth each other. The company sees the employees as no-good, useless takers and the employees see the company as some kind of an idiot who doesn't know what it's doing. All of this pent-up energy of anger, fear, and frustration gets vented at the coffee machines and so-called management meetings (where everyone figures out how to better control the slaves and get them to do what you want). What a *wonderful* situation!

Doesn't it just make you think of forests, trees and animals and the absolute power and beauty of the awesome interstellar realm of planets and stars and how your incredible existence here fits right in with all of that? Well, not really. This artificial kingdom exists completely in a void as though nothing else exists, save its own self. The people who work for this completely unnatural kingdom of reality are so depleted and so pained when they leave that job, that they can only go home or find somewhere else to hide and drown their sorrows in television, drugs, alcohol, or the like. Why the need for these three entities in the artificial world? Because they serve to repress emotion and prevent one from feeling the pain of a totally unnatural existence. In short, they render a person completely unconscious so that he or she is able to continue the denial and pretend that everything is just fine.

Let us now examine exactly how this artificial kingdom gets created through the reverse-flow energy of everyone affected by this Absence.

We will start by showing how a radiating flow of energy influences a person's experience of themselves and how they contribute to the planet. Let's look at Diagram A at the bottom of this page.

We can see from the drawing that the first impulse of Omnipresence strikes this person's heart via their infinite human presence. In that experience they are immediately fulfilled and filled with a powerful sense of who they are. They experience "I am", a condition of total fulfillment, total love, security, and presence. Now look at Diagram B at the top of the opposite page.

In this drawing, that first impulse of Omnipresence now moves from the heart into the mind, to fill that mind with presence and light. This person now experiences the illuminating power of creation and creative energy. There is an overall sense of knowingness shared between their heart and mind, or emo-

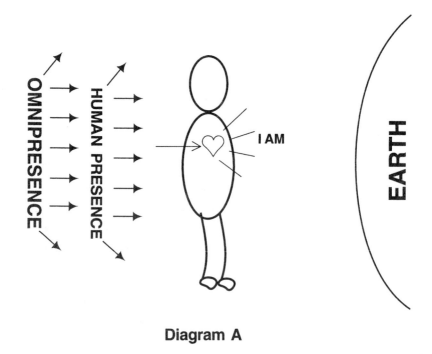

Diagram A

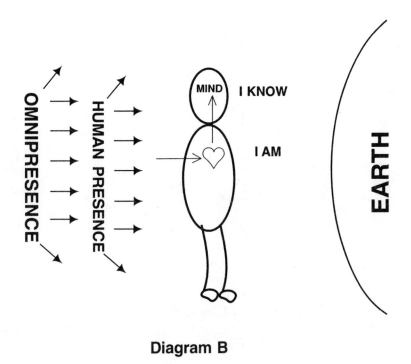

Diagram B

tions and thoughts. They experience a tremendous sense of certainty in that deep inner knowing that can only come from Omnipresence itself. Their mind is filled with the genius of bold, new, illuminating ideas. Now let's move on to Diagram C at the top of the next page.

In this illustration, the impulse of Omnipresence has moved from the mind into the entire body and ignites the whole system with the exhilarating feeling of purpose and intention. The body is now prepared, energized, and enlivened to act. Our bodies love this feeling of being alive to contribute something! They are completely fulfilled by this radiating presence of love, surrender to it effortlessly in their natural state, and ultimately experience the supreme bliss of allowing that energy to flow through them. Incidentally, it is the flow of this radiating, infi-

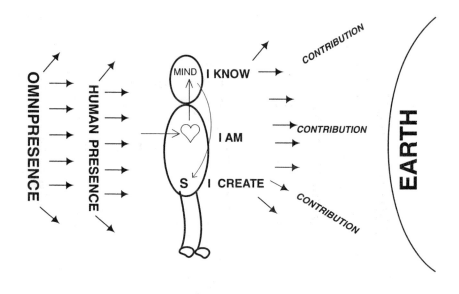

Diagram C

nite power of love and Omnipresence that can actually transform a finite, physical body into one of divine immortality and infinite nature.

Now the miracle is complete. This person exists as a divine manifestation of Omnipresent love and is fully able to accommodate the flow of that love through their infinite, human presence upon this planetary sphere. Their entire self, physical body included, exists solely for the purpose of contributing a radiating flow of creative energy and a manifestation of Love onto the earth itself. They are a link, a bridge if you will, between the infinite Universe and earth itself. A human being in the ultimate sense, is perfectly designed to exist as a vehicle through which the Universe itself can touch any planet and enact itself accordingly upon that planet for purposes of creative evolution of that entire sphere of life.

Now let's see what happens when the absence enters into

the consciousness of the incredible human being. Let's start with Diagram D at the bottom of the page.

In this illustration, the principle of the Absence has infiltrated the human dimension of consciousness on this planet and fully engaged itself at the point within this person where they would normally experience Omnipresence.

Instead of the experience of fulfillment produced by Love and Omnipresence, there is only a void. A sense of nothingness. Do you know what that void engenders in that person? That's right! A *question*. The question manifests as "Who am I ?" Let's look at Diagram E on the next page.

In this drawing, the mind also waits for an infinite impulse of light and divine brilliance, yet receives nothing. In that emptiness, it, too, has a question. The question for the mind is "Why am I here?" The mind experiences no ability to fulfill its infinite purpose, which is to create and *see* creation based upon that infinite impulse of presence that it receives from the heart.

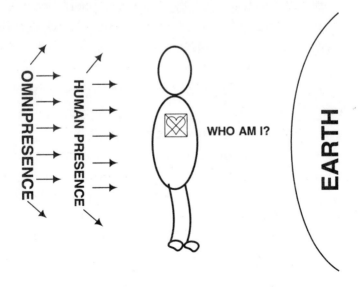

Diagram D

133

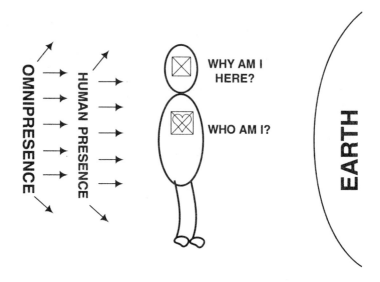

Diagram E

The mind does not have a clue about what creation is intended to flow through it from the Universe itself, because there is no impulse to tell it. It awaits that impulse, and experiences only a void. (Which ultimately makes it frantic and anxiety-ridden, causing it to jump all over the place trying to take control of things, as the "weight of the world" rests upon its shoulders, since it must now think of everything alone.) Let us now observe Diagram F at the top of the next page.

In this illustration, the body, too, awaits that divine impulse of Omnipresence to radiate through it from the mind in the form of thought, which is ultimately intended to activate the body into knowing what to do next in the form of action to manifest that creation. The body awaits a true impulse of power and enlightened thought to motivate it into action and receives nothing and very little energy, as well. A question arises throughout the physical experience of this person. The ques-

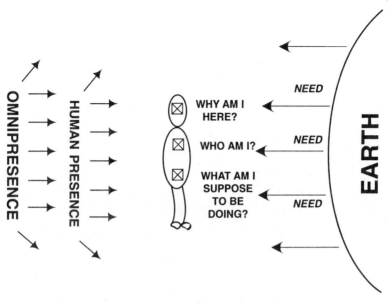

Diagram F

tion is, "What am I supposed to be doing?"

Now we see how each of these three aspects of this person receive little or no impulse of power, light, love, and truth. No experience of Omnipresence flows through this entity and instead they are left feeling separated and alone, in the company of this void or Absence. The void engenders a multitude of questions within them, the main ones being, "Who am I?" "Why am I here?" and "What am I supposed to be doing?" Because these questions stem from a void, they are also simultaneously accompanied by a tremendous *need*. Which need? A need for answers in order that this individual might survive. This person now has a tremendous need for the *external* environment to provide them with everything, in the way of fulfillment, knowing, and purpose, because the *real* source of those experiences is felt to be extinct within them, as a result of the Absence's resistance to Omnipresence.

Their need is great because to them their survival depends upon those needs being met. Were they existing in the full and radiating flow of Omnipresence, the power of that life force would sustain them completely and they would spend their life *living* and giving as opposed to existing from the fearful place of survival and need.

That ever-pressing need in them now manifests in a powerful reverse-flow of energy which depletes the surrounding environment, *takes* from it (all justified because it's for survival, of course) and gives rise to the most bizarre creations of reverse-flow power ever conceived by anyone.

Let us now examine how humanity's reverse-flow need and fundamental questions about themselves, arising from the existence of this void, bring forth the beginnings of institutions that have created the artificial kingdom. Let's observe another series of diagrams.

In our first drawing, which is Diagram G, below, the reverse-

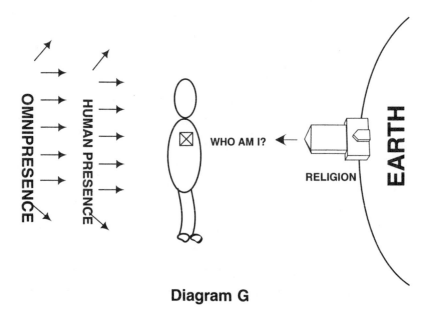

Diagram G

flow need generated by the question "Who am I ?" which arises from the void, brings forth an artificial, conceptual answer to that question which is sourced externally, to substitute for the missing experience within. It is no accident that religion would spring up to answer this question, because "Who am I?" is a matter of the heart, the original place from which we experience our oneness with Omnipresence, which is ultimately who we are. The absence of this experience is deemed a "spiritual" matter that exists *between* humanity and God (both of which are now experienced as separate), and the religions appoint themselves to be the "official" institution that will now take over for the missing experience, and "decide" what the answer is in an artificial, conceptual way. In a total reverse-flow of experience, the religions now give people the answer to that question in an artificial way, that comes from outside of them, in a way that can never fulfill, because fulfillment *only* comes from within, and cannot be controlled by outside institutions of any kind. In other words, the religions will now conceptually *tell* people what their missing experience is and expect that to be a fine substitute for reality itself. Because the religions arise in response to a reverse-flow need, they exist in many ways to dominate humanity's experience of God and decide for them what that experience will be. This scenario provides a perfect example of what it means to create an illusion that a need is being met.

Let us now take a look at Diagram H on the next page.

In this drawing, we can see the institution that has sprung up in response to the question, "Why am I here?" You guessed it. School. The great programming institutions of the human mind. It is assumed that an empty mind needs a lot of answers, and to that mind, it is indeed the case. School, in many cases, attempts to dominate the minds of those who attend by decid-

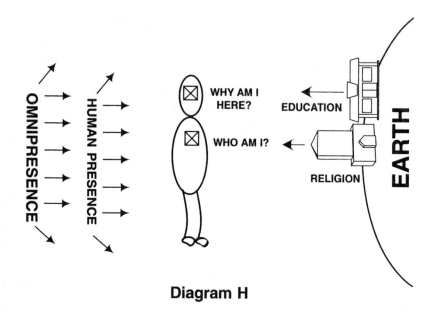

Diagram H

ing *for* those people what shall go in their minds. The institution of schooling directly answers the question "Why am I here?" by engaging its participants in at least 12 to 16 years of "job training" which will take place over the course of every individual's natural childhood and growth into adulthood. The reason this takes so long is that it is completely unnatural for any wild, free-spirited, creative human being to spend their entire time upon this earth in a "job" earning a mere pittance to survive on. But because the stated purpose for these people in the artificial world is to have this "job" nonetheless, it is worth every grueling year of effort, throughout childhood, to program them to think that they feel comfortable in that existence. Think about it. School exactly replicates the adult version of 9 to 5 (or 8 to 5, these days). It goes Monday through Friday, just like a job, and starts early in the morning, just like a job. In school you have a teacher who tells you what to do and gives you tasks to perform and later on, in your job, that person will be replaced by a boss who will also tell you what to do and give you tasks to perform. In school you are rewarded with grades for following instructions and doing what you're told, and later, in a job, you will be rewarded with a paycheck for following instructions and doing what you're told. Oh, and by the way, they also make those school rooms resemble offices as best they can, so you can easily slip right into a job with hardly knowing the difference. In school you have your little desk, which will later be replaced by a bigger desk in your office. They also make sure that schools have those awful fluorescent lights so that your eyes will be used to the same when it's time to go to your office. And, of course, schools have lunch breaks and recess (because children have to be weaned from moving around too much), while later in your job you'll have a lunch break and coffee breaks. So school is the big answer to the large question of "Why am I here?" and will train and program you for the incredible, long haul of your "purpose" on this earth which is to be a worker, get a job, and live only to survive.

And now we shall move ahead to our final illustration, Diagram I, at the top of the next page.

In this final drawing, we see the last institution to spring up in response to the question, "What am I supposed to be doing?" which is the institution of government and the law. The institution of government is basically there to tell everyone what to do and to keep everybody physically in line. This institution would be an absolutely obvious manifestation in response to the need of millions of physically existing individuals who haven't got a clue as to what to do with themselves from an integrated, harmonious place of Love that stems from their natural place in the Universe itself. They can't know this,

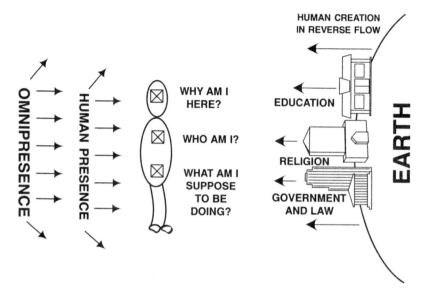

Diagram I

because they have no impulse of Omnipresent Love to tell them or motivate them on a physical level. Instead, they live in the fear produced by the void and will act out just about any scenario in the world of dominate/be dominated in order to survive. Of course it would be necessary in this scenario to create an artificial institution of government and law, to artificially control and dominate the actions of the people (with some limited bit of freedom, of course) and prevent them from killing each other and themselves! So government exists as an artificial "replacement" for the missing experience of God and Omnipresence which is the real power that "rules" the Universe, as they say. The difference between government and God, of course, is that Omnipresence exists in full command of the entire cosmos, because it *is* that cosmos, and manifests solely as an expression of love. Government, on the other hand, being a product of the Absence and the void and the fear which that absence induces, works *against* the people by dominating them and does so through fear, intimidation, and threats.

So these three institutions arise and are created out of a desperate human need which comes out of the fear experienced from the void produced by the Absence, where Omnipresence can no longer be felt. All of them exist in a total reverse-flow, deplete the planet and never ultimately fulfill the needs of the people. This is, in actuality, what keeps these institutions around and surviving. The illusion of needs being met by artificially devised substitutes for Omnipresence, is exactly what the source of fear ultimately thrives on.

Chapter 10

Human Beings In Relationship

Human beings, in their natural state, are meant to relate to each other out of love. Unfortunately, on our planet, we relate to each other mostly out of need. But this seems obvious, does it not, now that you are understanding more and more about the source of fear? Fear produces need and fear is what it feels like when you find that you have no experience of Omnipresence. Let us add one point here. We are not living in a condition where our level of experience of life and Love measures at an absolute zero. If this were the case, we wouldn't survive. This brings up a very interesting point. In a general sense, we mostly tend to experience only the level of life force necessary to enable us to live in this world and survive. And that includes the amount of love, as well. It exists at a bare minimum. Again, just enough to survive. This is because, as you remember, survival has become the clearly stated purpose.

Now some of you might be thinking, "But that's not true! I have a lot of love in my life." Well, first of all, we are talking about the overall human condition, in a general sense, and secondly, you might be very surprised to discover how cleverly and imperceptibly need often masquerades as love. Let's observe the simple diagram, Diagram A, on the next page.

In this drawing, we see where the Absence has infiltrated the human experience. The missing experience of Omnipresence now produces a tremendous need. The void produces a reverse-flow of energy, which is a manifestation of that need... This person needs a certain experience, although they don't know what that experience is, because they don't have it! So

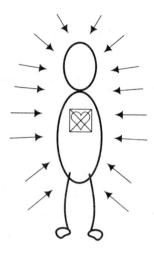

Diagram A

they will go out and try all sorts of different experiences trying to fill the void. The problem is, of course, that they can never fill that void from the outside. Yet the reverse-flow energy that is set up from within, turns their attention away from surrender and letting go to the flow of an infinite experience that is sourced from within, to looking outside of themselves for that fulfillment. So how do you think this reverse-flow of energy affects all of their relationships, when their focus in life is filling that need? Look at the direction of the arrows. Are they going outward, or pointing inward? They are pointing inward, of course, in this person's total preoccupation with filling themselves.

Let's look at Diagram B on the opposite page.

This drawing shows that the *source* of love is Omnipresence. Love is a *real* energy, you see. It has substance, power, and impact. People often mistakenly equate love with behavior.

Let's say that your friend calls you up and says, "Hi! I'm moving today. Would you come over and help me pack and

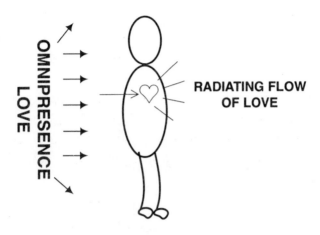

Diagram B

load the moving truck?" You, of course, are simply leaping out of your seat in joy to have been given this wonderful opportunity! Well, not really. Actually, the truth is that you had other plans. You were planning to go on a wonderful picnic with some friends and were really looking forward to relaxing on your day off. *But*! You feel *guilty*. You really *should* help your friend out. After all, what if *you* were in a jam someday? Wouldn't you want someone to help you, too? Gosh, if you *don't* help your friend, God just might *put* you in a real jam one day, with no help, just to teach you a lesson. Maybe you better go, just to be safe. So, out of fear, you say, "Well, um, I did have other plans, but um, I guess I *could* cancel them. It wasn't that important anyway."

Your friend says, "Gee, *thanks*! You're a *great* friend!" So you call up your other friends, tell them you can't make it to the picnic, and by now you're feeling really angry. Your whole day has been ruined and you're not going to get another break until your next day off.

Is this love? Of course not. Look at the emotions. Fear, guilt, and anger. It *doesn't matter* that you go over to your friend's house with a big smile on your face, acting as though everything is just great, when inside you're feeling completely resentful.

Yet people will say that this is love, when in truth it is just artificial behavior born out of fear and guilt, that is masquerading as love. What makes it artificial? The very fact that you have to *force* yourself to do it, when in truth, you really don't want to.

Let's look at another example. Have you heard of Mother Teresa? This woman has devoted her life to *loving* every human being on the face of the earth, particularly those who are starving, diseased, and living in absolutely unbearable poverty. She exists as a powerful force and an awesome presence, as tiny as she is and as *humble* as she is because what flows through her is the real power and presence of God itself. The Universe manifests untold benefits and healing to thousands of people all over the world through the hands of this small, little lady.

Can you imagine Mother Teresa getting up every morning, grumbling to herself, and feeling angry and resentful that she has to "help" these awful people when what she'd *really* rather be doing is watching television with her feet propped up on a chair, a beer in one hand, and the ever-present remote in the other? But alas, she's been *forced* to do this miserable work because she's a guilty, rotten sinner herself and God is likely to punish her "later on" if she doesn't drag herself out there one more day and act as though she loves these people. Well, this is hardly what happens. But if it did, would you say it was love just because she went out there anyway and *pretended* it was so?

Now many people would find this example to be laughable. "Mother Teresa would *never* act that way. *Her* love is *real!*" Yet most of the people on this earth *do* act this way and say it's real, even when it's not. "So what are we supposed to do?" you might say. "If everyone stopped pretending to be loving even when they're not, the whole world would fall apart! No one would ever do anything for anybody, everyone would be upset, and it would be a disaster!"

Well, even if that were to be the case, it only shows how much *real* love is truly missing from our experience. The answer is not to stop helping people and become truly mean to everyone saying, "Tough luck for you! I don't *feel* like helping you, so go away. I'm busy." We are not suggesting that you *affirm* the anger, and call that the truth. The truth is, you see, that we *are* truly loving, giving, and contributing people. We *adore* contributing, we love it, it is who we are and it totally, absolutely fulfills us beyond anything else in the Universe. But only if it comes from *real* love, which is always sourced in Omnipresence. So the key is to find out why that love is missing, cease to tolerate the Absence and its negative effect upon our experience, and do something about it, which is why you're reading this book. You already know why the love is missing. You have every right to feel intolerant of that principle because it is preventing you from experiencing the truth of who you really are, and you *can* do something about it by positioning yourself to have it eliminated, which is what we've been doing throughout the course of this book.

One of the most interesting things that people love to do on our wonderful planet earth, out of all of the need that is generated by this Absence, is to play what we call "The Happy Face Game." The happy face game is very interesting. All that you need in order to play is yourself, and literally everyone else

Diagram C

that you know. Here's how to play. The object of the game is to find a way to keep everybody smiling, whenever they look at you. Here's how it works. Let's look at the drawing above, Diagram C.

In this drawing, there you are in the middle, surrounded by all of your friends, family, and acquaintances. What you must now do is to "dance" a great dance and try to keep everyone you know smiling and approving of you, every single minute. What is the reason for this dance? Well, it's simple. It's done for the purpose of getting self-esteem! The only problem is that it's very difficult to keep dancing for *everyone*, all at the same time, and keep everybody happy all at the same time as well.

As you can see in the picture, this person is dancing very hard but only three people are smiling! No sooner does the person in the middle figure out the dance that one person over here wants them to do, thereby getting them to smile, when the guy on the other side starts feeling neglected and gets angry. By the time you're finished with this game, all you will want to do is collapse in bed from exhaustion! No one has ever succeeded at keeping everyone happy in their life, all of the time, by dancing just the right dance for everyone else.

And the game gets even *more* complicated, you see, because each of the characters in the circle is most likely playing the exact same game with everyone *they* know as well! And to them, *you* are one of the people in their audience. So what do you suppose all of this leads to when everyone is playing this game all at once? What it leads to is the most *immense*, complicated network of human beings manipulating, bartering, trading, politicing, and making social deals of every kind imaginable among themselves. A "bad day" is when this dancing network starts to collapse on your side of things and you're just not getting the feedback that you so desperately need to receive.

So where does this game come from? Once again, it comes from the need produced by the source of fear, that occurs when an individual is unable to experience the true power of who they really are. Without that experience, there is only a void in its place and that void produces anxiety, insecurity, and tremendous feelings of unworthiness or lack of self-esteem. The fear and insecurity which is produced by that missing experience is truly unbearable and a person will therefore feel compelled, as in so many of the examples in our last chapter, to seek an artificial substitute from outside of themselves. You see, the person in the middle of the circle is unable to experience self-love, because self-love is the experience of knowing Omnipresence experientially, experiencing that energy to be who you are, and thus loving yourself accordingly. You can't help but love yourself because you and Love are one and the same.

But as we've been saying over and over again, that experience *must* come from within, because Omnipresence is the *only* source of an experience of real Love, because it *is* Love, it is infinite, and it *is* everywhere, all at once. We can only know this power, which is likewise the power of who we are, from deep within our hearts.

The happy face game can never bring *real* love to anyone. It can only bring approval, which is an illusion of love and usually means that you are merely doing something which matches that other person's belief system, makes them feel comfortable with you, and therefore inspires them to give you some "good" feedback, because you have just affirmed for them that *their* beliefs are right. So for them, it's not really about you, anyway. In their own experience of reverse-flow and need, they can only approve of you for giving them the feedback that *they* need for themselves.

And the bottom line of this game is that, in reality, it is only another game of dominate/be dominated and manipulation. Why? Because in the happy face game what you are ultimately trying to do is manipulate the feelings of someone else to be what *you* want them to be for purposes of filling your own need.

Let's look at another famous game masquerading as love. We'll call it the do-gooder game. In this game, the do-gooder believes that he or she must help and rescue everyone else. On the surface, it looks as though do-gooders are these loving, caring, amazing people. But there's something a little bit aggravating about them, isn't there? They are incredibly *compulsive* about doing it. There's even a sense that they're not really responding to reality in their actions, because their actions are the same, all the time, in every situation. In this case, when the actions become repetitive and compulsive, with a need to react in the same way, regardless of the situation at hand, you can say that that person is dealing with a pattern. A pattern is something that happens unconsciously in a person's behavior, over and over again, that carries with it tremendous need and reverse-flow energy, causing that individual to believe that they simply *must* act on the basis of that pattern or they will not survive.

In the case of an artificial, do-gooder scenario, the do-gooder could be reacting to any number of needs—the need for approval, the need to feel more powerful, the need to keep everyone around them calm and stable (because they can't handle the emotions of other people), the need to be in control, a need to feel like a "good" person and thereby gain self-worth, the need to be liked, the list goes on and on....

Please do not interpret that we are saying that anyone who ever tries to help someone is responding artificially, out of a pattern of need. Of *course* we're not saying that. There are many occasions where people will do something for others out of sincere love and appreciation. We are simply saying that it is useful to know the difference between what is real and what isn't.

Let us now discuss some of the more dire consequences of having this absence infiltrate our human experience and how it affects our relationships with each other.

We will first discuss the notion of *power*. As a result of the existence of the source of fear in our planetary dimension of reality, we have collectively acquired a notion of power that exists in our consciousness as an exact mirror image of this absence, in human manifestation. That notion of power is based upon the belief that power is measured by one's ability to dominate. *True* power is the power to live and to express oneself accordingly. Ultimately it manifests as the power of Omnipresence manifesting as Love and unlimited creativity. False power is that which the Absence engages in its basic principle of survival which is the power to dominate the truth by resisting it. In dominating the truth, the Absence attempts to dominate life because Omnipresence *is* life and the source of life, as well. Life and Omnipresence are perceived as a threat to its existence, which they are, because in that presence, no void can exist.

So how does this manifest in human terms? It manifests as anything and everything that we might do which goes against life itself. In its most dire example, it has manifested as the action of human beings deliberately killing other human beings, and this, dear friends, has been going on for thousands of years. We have over the ages killed and wiped out literally countless millions of our human selves in acts of hatred, vengeance, and war. When all else fails, just threaten to kill somebody and you'll probably get your way. The greatest science of technology on our planet is the science of weapons designed to destroy life. We are always in a mode of destruction and see that as an answer to everything. To the Absence, killing represents the ultimate illusion of power because it represents the greatest act of going against life, which is Omnipresence, the very truth which it attempts to resist as its core principle of existence. So to this phenomenon, killing, repression, and domination of everything is the only possible way that it can manifest its so-called "power" because that is the only thing which it is capable of in accordance with its design.

Let's now examine how nations are created. Do you think that all of those little lines drawn all over the maps really exist? Of course they don't. Go up in space and see it for yourself. Or better yet, take a ride in an airplane. You still won't see them. They are completely made up, fictitious, hallucinatory lines. What are they comprised of? Dominate/be dominated of course. Every nation that exists in this world came into being through an act of domination. It started with a desire to dominate the land, the earth itself. Those lines were established through acts of killing and war. There has been so much human bloodshed over the ages by acts of human hands, that one could not even begin to fathom it all. And yet we take this so for granted. We *assume* that all of this killing somehow equates the power to survive. But survival is not living, as we said before. It is, in reality, death, because its source exists in an absolute lack of truth, life, and love.

So killing fulfills a need, yes. A need to survive and keep life out, which is the need of the Absence, a phenomenon existing as the only true form of death.

Acting on behalf of this phenomenon will always invoke death in some form, as death supplies it with a mirror-image of itself.

Chapter 11

Patterns

We will now discuss how the existence of the source of fear tracks patterns in our human behavior which exactly replicate its fundamental principles of design. What are patterns? Patterns are those annoying, aggravating, frustrating actions of behavior, thoughts, feelings, and emotions that we tend to repeat over and over again, in spite of the fact that they often cause pain, inhibit our expression, and bring mostly unwanted results.

Have you ever tried to break a pattern? It's not easy, is it? It seems that it should be, doesn't it? After all, it seems that if it's something you're doing (or not doing) that you don't like and don't wish to continue, then you should just be able to *stop*, right? Wrong! So why is it that something that should be so simple and easy is often so incredibly difficult?

In order to understand the answer to that question, we must begin by viewing our wonderful, human bodies in a more expanded way. First of all, *you* are not your body. Your body is comprised of the elements of the earth and actually serves as a magnificent vehicle through which *you* can exist here on this planet. Okay, so then who are *you*? You are, in truth, the most amazing human presence that exists as a full manifestation of Omnipresence in human form. You are infinite, immortal, and completely unbound by this seemingly finite, planetary sphere. But nonetheless, you *do* have a purpose in being here and in order for the earth to benefit from your wonderful human presence you must have a body which can allow you to touch the earth, feel it, and know it in a completely physical way. This

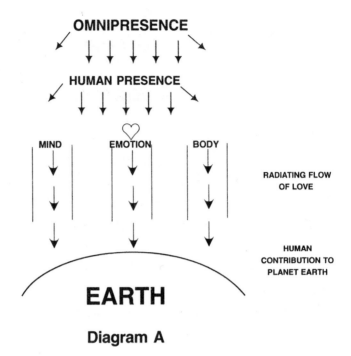

Diagram A

means that your body will have to be of the earth and at the same time of the Universe—divine in nature, to allow you to be here and contribute something as who you truly are.

Thus your body possesses a magnificent, physical spectrum of energy and possibility, comprised of emotional, mental, and physical "channels," if you will, which allows your full presence to manifest on this earth. The important thing to understand about these physical, mental, and emotional channels which comprise your physical human body is that they are specifically designed to conduct *only* a radiating flow of love, energy, and Omnipresence. They were not made to conduct energy flowing in reverse, and when it does, it has a devastating effect on the entire system, and mostly on you in terms of your experience on this planet of who you are.

Let us look at Diagram A at the top of this page.

This diagram shows Omnipresence in a radiating flow manifesting as human presence (you), also in a radiating flow, and then shows how that energy radiates in the same flow throughout your entire system (emotion, mind, and body) to be expressed outwardly, in love, on the planet itself.

The important thing to recognize here is that all of the energy is flowing in the *same direction*, from the source of everything, all the way through, until it reaches the planet. Nature, in its infinite intelligence tends to design itself with consistency in accordance with the greater whole. And if everything is indeed a manifestation of Omnipresence, which it is, then every manifestation of that Intelligence will be consistent with its flow of energy.

So what happens when the Absence enters into the picture? Let's observe Diagram B, below, and find out.

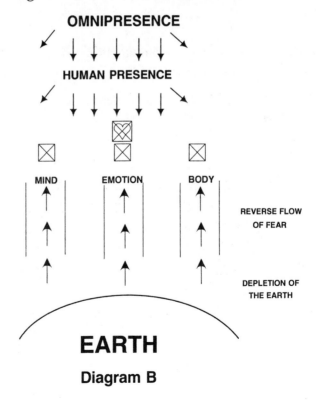

OMNIPRESENCE

HUMAN PRESENCE

MIND EMOTION BODY

REVERSE FLOW
OF FEAR

DEPLETION OF
THE EARTH

EARTH

Diagram B

In Diagram B, the Absence has entered into the picture and is setting up a reverse-flow of energy inside the entire system, which causes this person's actions to deplete the earth rather than contribute to it. Notice that the arrows in this person's system are pointing in the *opposite* direction of Omnipresence and Love.

Now let's look at the next drawing, Diagram C, to get a closer look at how this affects the human system itself.

As you observe this drawing , below, you will see a diagram of some "valves" existing within the human system. Here, again, we have a problem with our language. In reality, there are no valves, per se, but there *is* a factor inside of us that replicates what these valves are modeling for you. The problem is that our language does not contain any word or concept to

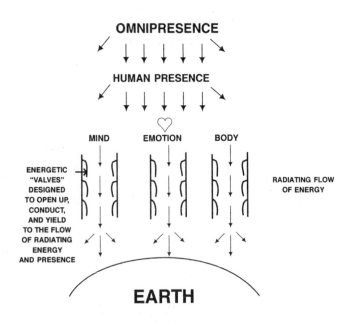

Diagram C

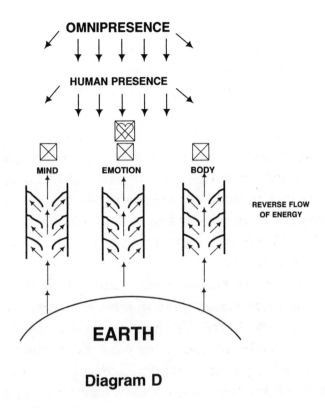

Diagram D

adequately describe what this factor is, so we will therefore use the simple concept of these valves to make the point.

These valves (or the real factor that exists inside of us) have to do with our ability to surrender and experience the joy and bliss of that letting go. It is ultimately what allows us to become one with the Universe on every single level of our existence.

Now let's see how a reverse-flow affects these "valves." Look at Diagram D, at the top of the page.

In this drawing, you can see the energy flowing backwards, in reverse, through this person's entire system. The "valves" cannot yield in the direction of a reverse-flow, because magnetically they are not made for it. In fact, they actually get in the way of that energy moving backwards and this causes the energy to collect behind them. The energy then begins to accumulate in this person's system as old, unreleased experiences which ultimately form patterns.

Let's look at Diagram E, opposite, to see how this happens.

This drawing illustrates another very significant point. Where the absence does not exist, a human being's experience of life is completely sourced in Omnipresence and Love. When the absence comes into play, however, that changes completely. Now that person's experience of life is sourced from everything that happens outside of themselves.

The effect that this actually has is fascinating in terms of how we perceive time.

The normal, human perception of time in a condition of Omnipresence and radiating flow, is to experience life in the eternal Now. In truth, there is no time, really. All experiences are ultimately sourced in the Now. Everything that we know experientially emanates from each and every moment of now. As we said earlier, many people attempt to experience this Now through meditations and the like. But try this. Try *not* to exist right now. It can't be done. If we were to ask you at *any moment*, any moment at all, "what time is it?" you'd have to, in truth, answer *"right now."* Try to experience anything other than "right now." You cannot do it. Ultimately, you don't have to work hard at all to be in the Now. If you look at your experience, you can't get out of it!

Now some people will say, "Wait just a minute, here. What about my memory? I remember *lots* of things that happened before!" Well, look at your *experience of remembering* something. Your experience of memory always happens *right now*. There is absolutely no proof of any kind whatsoever that anything ever existed prior to this exact moment of now.

Then, of course, someone else will say, "Oh, yeah? I have

① HUMAN SYSTEM IN ITS NATURAL STATE

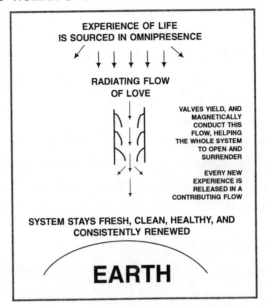

EXPERIENCE OF LIFE
IS SOURCED IN OMNIPRESENCE

RADIATING FLOW
OF LOVE

VALVES YIELD, AND
MAGNETICALLY
CONDUCT THIS
FLOW, HELPING
THE WHOLE SYSTEM
TO OPEN AND
SURRENDER

EVERY NEW
EXPERIENCE IS
RELEASED IN A
CONTRIBUTING FLOW

SYSTEM STAYS FRESH, CLEAN, HEALTHY, AND
CONSISTENTLY RENEWED

EARTH

② HUMAN SYSTEM WITH THE ABSENCE

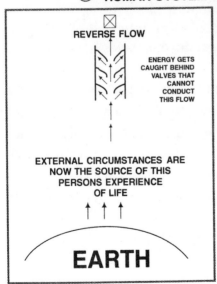

REVERSE FLOW

ENERGY GETS
CAUGHT BEHIND
VALVES THAT
CANNOT
CONDUCT
THIS FLOW

EXTERNAL CIRCUMSTANCES ARE
NOW THE SOURCE OF THIS
PERSONS EXPERIENCE
OF LIFE

EARTH

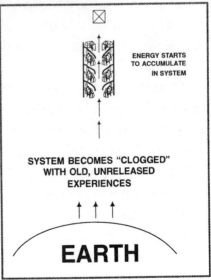

ENERGY STARTS
TO ACCUMULATE
IN SYSTEM

SYSTEM BECOMES "CLOGGED"
WITH OLD, UNRELEASED
EXPERIENCES

EARTH

Diagram E

proof. I have *photographs* of things that happened before. That *proves* that there was indeed a past." Well, look at your experience. Your experience of seeing, feeling, and physically touching those photographs can only happen right now. If someone asked you "What time is it?" while you're holding that photograph of the so-called past in your hand you'd have to answer "right now." The photograph itself can only exist in the now. Gee, for all we know someone could have installed a little "microchip" in our brain that takes everything we experience now, attaches a little story to it, and creates the illusion of past and future just to give us a false way to understand our existence. If that thought is too much for you, then just pretend it's a joke!

Let us look at the illustrations on the opposite page to see how time exists in a radiating flow and then in reverse-flow.

The first drawing, Diagram F, represents the experience of a human being in a normal flow of radiating time and space, all emanating from the eternal Now.

Can you see in this next drawing, Diagram G, how inappropriate experiences collect and produce a "layering" of the so-called past? What makes them inappropriate for this individual, is that they are not even necessarily his or her experiences! They can be anything at all that happens in the world around them, having to do with other people, other circumstances, or whatever. There is no guarantee, in a reverse-flow reality of *what* you will absorb into your system. It all depends on what's happening around you. Like it or not, it will all go into your experience.

If you remember the "suction" effect produced by the Absence, you can start to understand why it is so difficult to let go of a pattern, or to let go of old, past experiences. No matter how hard you try, that invisible suction keeps it held inside of

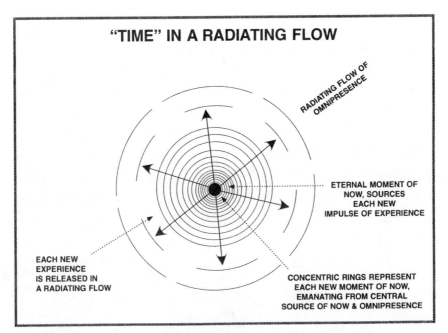

"TIME" IN A RADIATING FLOW

RADIATING FLOW OF OMNIPRESENCE

ETERNAL MOMENT OF NOW, SOURCES EACH NEW IMPULSE OF EXPERIENCE

EACH NEW EXPERIENCE IS RELEASED IN A RADIATING FLOW

CONCENTRIC RINGS REPRESENT EACH NEW MOMENT OF NOW, EMANATING FROM CENTRAL SOURCE OF NOW & OMNIPRESENCE

Diagram F

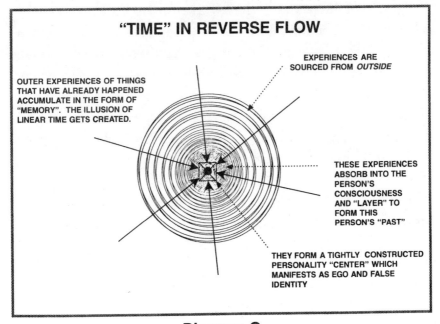

"TIME" IN REVERSE FLOW

EXPERIENCES ARE SOURCED FROM *OUTSIDE*

OUTER EXPERIENCES OF THINGS THAT HAVE ALREADY HAPPENED ACCUMULATE IN THE FORM OF "MEMORY". THE ILLUSION OF LINEAR TIME GETS CREATED.

THESE EXPERIENCES ABSORB INTO THE PERSON'S CONSCIOUSNESS AND "LAYER" TO FORM THIS PERSON'S "PAST"

THEY FORM A TIGHTLY CONSTRUCTED PERSONALITY "CENTER" WHICH MANIFESTS AS EGO AND FALSE IDENTITY

Diagram G

you, just like a powerful vacuum hose would hold a thin piece of paper and other pieces of paper layered on top of that.

Sometimes people get so fed up with their recurring patterns, that they will attend workshops, lectures, and methods specifically designed to support personal growth. While they are there, they might have a powerful experience, go home all excited that they have finally released something, and three days later it's back *again*. Does this mean that the workshop didn't work? No! What it usually means is that the source of fear continued to keep that person gripped in a reverse-flow of energy and even if that individual experienced a momentary release of something in their past, it was only a matter of time before that pattern would find its way back into their consciousness.

Which brings us to a *very important* point: The final elimination of the source of fear will *not* get rid of the patterns. But it *will* get rid of the source of the reverse-flow suction that is holding those patterns in place. Once the source of fear is eliminated, your whole way of dealing with patterns can completely change. Instead of trying to overcome them, work around them, function in spite of them, go "beyond" them, etc. you can take an entirely different approach. You will actually be able, with conscious effort, to *transmute* whatever patterns you desire, and cause them to disappear *forever*, because you will not have the source of fear there "gluing" them to you with that incredible, reverse-flow suction. You will have a sufficient amount of presence available to you to transmute unwanted patterns in the powerful, transmutational energy of Omnipresent Love.

Let us now take a look at one more thing, and that is the false personality and how it is formed.

Let's start by observing the next diagram, Diagram H, which

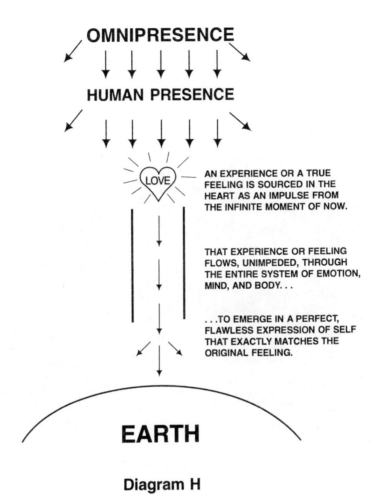

OMNIPRESENCE

HUMAN PRESENCE

LOVE — AN EXPERIENCE OR A TRUE FEELING IS SOURCED IN THE HEART AS AN IMPULSE FROM THE INFINITE MOMENT OF NOW.

THAT EXPERIENCE OR FEELING FLOWS, UNIMPEDED, THROUGH THE ENTIRE SYSTEM OF EMOTION, MIND, AND BODY. . .

. . .TO EMERGE IN A PERFECT, FLAWLESS EXPRESSION OF SELF THAT EXACTLY MATCHES THE ORIGINAL FEELING.

EARTH

Diagram H

illustrates the entire human system in a radiating flow.

This drawing illustrates the perfectly authentic flow of human self-expression, when unimpeded by the Absence.

Now let's look at what happens when that impulse of experience or feeling tries to flow through a human system that has been affected by the Absence or source of fear.

Please observe Diagram I on the next page.

Does this drawing remind you of all the times in your life that you felt one thing and did another? How about the times

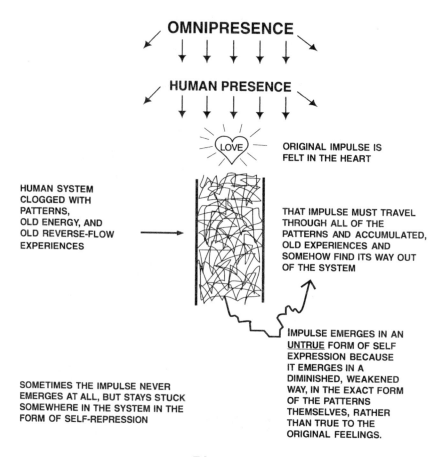

OMNIPRESENCE

HUMAN PRESENCE

LOVE — ORIGINAL IMPULSE IS FELT IN THE HEART

HUMAN SYSTEM CLOGGED WITH PATTERNS, OLD ENERGY, AND OLD REVERSE-FLOW EXPERIENCES

THAT IMPULSE MUST TRAVEL THROUGH ALL OF THE PATTERNS AND ACCUMULATED, OLD EXPERIENCES AND SOMEHOW FIND ITS WAY OUT OF THE SYSTEM

IMPULSE EMERGES IN AN UNTRUE FORM OF SELF EXPRESSION BECAUSE IT EMERGES IN A DIMINISHED, WEAKENED WAY, IN THE EXACT FORM OF THE PATTERNS THEMSELVES, RATHER THAN TRUE TO THE ORIGINAL FEELINGS.

SOMETIMES THE IMPULSE NEVER EMERGES AT ALL, BUT STAYS STUCK SOMEWHERE IN THE SYSTEM IN THE FORM OF SELF-REPRESSION

Diagram I

that you felt a powerful expression welling up inside of you and when you went to say or do something about it, the words and actions in no way matched what you were really feeling or experiencing? Have you ever felt incredibly frustrated that your so-called personality expression in no way matches the truth of who you know yourself to be?

The reason for all of the above is that the accumulated energy of old, unreleased experiences are stuck in your system and clogging your perception, making it impossible for you to express yourself in a natural, authentic way. Because this stuff is "stuck" in one position, you find yourself doing, thinking, saying, and feeling the same stuff over and over and over again, even though life goes on in an attempted evolutionary flow. This is what is known as living through your patterns instead of being in the Now.

The false identity is comprised of an identification with these old experiences, thus producing a false-personality expression which is actually an expression of the patterns themselves.

Let's look at the next diagram, Diagram J, which shows a rather humorous display of two false personalities interacting with each other.

In this picture, each person believes themselves to be the sum total of all of their past experiences. When asked to talk about themselves, they will automatically pull out the "files" of past experiences which they believe that the other person most wants to hear.

So the false identity is comprised of all of the things that have happened to a person, to the extent which that person

FALSE PERSONALITY
WALKING - TALKING FILES

Diagram J

identifies with them. The false personality is the artificial expression of a person who believes themselves to be those things.

All in all, the Absence creates a totally distorted picture of ourselves and alters our perception of life in such a way that we believe ourselves to be the sum total of our past experiences, our negative, reverse-flow patterns, and all of the other stuff that has accumulated "in time" within our human systems. The grief that this causes internally is immense because it causes human beings to feel as though they have lost themselves and don't ever get a chance to truly live.

Chapter 12

Summary

We have now taken a substantial amount of time describing the source of fear, its origins, how it is structured, and exactly how it has affected us and our planet for literally thousands of years.

The only question now to ask yourself is, do you want to have this phenomenon eliminated from within yourself? To a lot of people that might sound just too easy, too simple. "How can you talk about just eliminating it? Shouldn't it be more difficult than that?" you might ask. "Shouldn't we have to overcome it or do battle with it or something like that?" Well, no. Actually, you've probably already been doing those things for most of your life without realizing it. And it doesn't work, does it? The more you try to fight it, resist it, and/or overcome it, the worse it gets. Why? Well, very simply because those very actions and attitudes are actually a product of the thing itself. So by "fighting" it, you actually give it more fuel.

Fortunately, there's a much better way and one that is totally effective. The only problem is that you might possibly think it's too easy! But it is easy, because you've already done your part in this process. "What do you mean we've already done our part?" you might be saying. Well, remember that your part was simply to read the book from cover to cover and allow yourself the experience of whatever the process of reading generated for you. If *that* sounds too easy, then remember that, in truth you have been preparing for this for your whole life. And likewise, the collective humanity, of which you are indeed a part, has been preparing for this for thousands of years and evolving to a point, over all that time, where it would be possible to recognize this phenomenon for what it is and cease to identify with it. For that has been the biggest problem all along, you see. Humanity's staunch position that all of this negative behavior is just a "part of life" and a "part of who we are" has been the single, greatest obstacle to us having the opportunity to have the problem eliminated, because that act of identifying with it would prevent us from being able to see it for what it is. And if we can't "see" it, then we can't support its elimination because we don't even know what we're supporting.

The religions have not helped in this regard because they have only supported the theory that all of this trouble is due to bad behavior on our part and the reason that we're suffering so is because "God" is punishing us for being sinners. This attitude and system of belief in no way empowers us to be able to take a stand in our own lives, say "Enough!" and fully intend to experience the final elimination of the source of fear.

Instead, this belief only causes us to feel guilty and deserving of the pain. What is guilt after all? Guilt is simply the act of thinking negative thoughts against yourself, which usually fall under one of two categories—bad, stupid, or both. Guilt is clearly an emotion that is generated by the source of fear, because it goes against yourself. And the irony in the whole thing is that if you indeed did perform some "wrong" action that you are feeling very guilty about, it no doubt happened because of the existence of the same phenomenon.

You see, once you really "get it" that this phenomenon is *not* you, because it is *not* Omnipresence, life, or anything else for that matter, everything will change. This phenomenon is the consumate "I am *not*," remember? Once you truly recognize this, you will experience tremendous freedom in that realization alone, and although that realization does not constitute the *elimination* of that phenomenon, it does make it extraordinarily easy to have it done because you are not hanging on to it anymore thinking that it's "you." The Universe is now able to act quickly on your behalf and create exactly the right synergistic arrangement of energy in combination with the forces of Nature and evolution, for you to have this phenomenon eliminated from within yourself, once and for all, for good. Isn't that wonderful?

For all of this time that we've been waiting for help, the truth is that the help has been here all along, poised and ready to assist us, from the moment that we first requested it. But first we had to be helped to a position of being able to see that it's not us, and stop identifying with it.

For those of you who might be harboring the belief that if the source of fear has found its way into our consciousness, then that must mean that "God wants it that way" and we probably "shouldn't be tampering with that" then look at it this way. Nature, in a huge, inter-Universal sense, is wild, free, and powerfully volatile in its constant generation of creation itself. It creates with supreme abandon and with an unlimited expansion of life and energy. It is also self-correcting the moment that anything is even remotely out of alignment. We are no exception to that! Our lives exist in the context of all life and of the Universe itself. We are a part of that great and powerful sea of ever-expanding energy. All that we have to do is surrender to that and allow the Universe to do its powerful, wonderful, and wholly awesome work which includes restoring ourselves and our planet and all of our experiences as a humanity back into a natural state.

Now let us address one final point here. Many times, after

hearing all that we have spoken about in this book, people will very much feel a desire to experience the final elimination of the source of fear for themselves. Yet there could be a certain amount of confusion about it because the mind, at this point, will commonly manifest thoughts like, "Oh, well, this will work for everyone else, but never for me." Or, "This just doesn't seem possible. What if it doesn't work?" Basically, all of these thoughts are simply manifesting as doubt, which due to the existence of the source of fear, is an exceedingly common human experience every time we try to move forward in life. Another thing that people commonly experience at this point is apprehension or anxiety. The mind wants to blow the whole thing way out of proportion and make it such a big deal that the thought of eliminating the source of fear becomes a totally intimidating idea! This perspective is way out of balance with the truth, because the experience of the final elimination of the source of fear can truly be approached as the most natural, obvious, and simple thing to do. It can be approached in a very calm and very simple way. It really is "no big deal" and later on we'll tell you why.

The important thing to remember is that Nature has designed this process to fully accommodate all of these disorienting thoughts and emotions of doubt, fear, and anxiety. These things often arise when it is time to eliminate the source of fear, because they are actually a product of that phenomenon itself. Because the source of fear exists in a state of total survival, it will often intensify greatly in your experience of it as you come closer and closer to having it eliminated. So the main thing here is not to worry or be concerned if you have these thoughts and feelings because the process itself can easily include all of that and work just fine regardless of whether they are there or not.

The only thing that you really need at this point in order to experience the final elimination of the source of fear is simply the *desire* to have it happen for you. If that desire is there and you are sincere about wanting it done, then that is quite literally all that you need. Isn't that wonderful? The wonderful thing about this next part of the process, which is the actual process by which you have an opportunity to experience the final elimination of the source of fear for yourself, is that at this point, you *can't mess it up*. Isn't that great? We are so used to doing things where the entire thing depends on us and on our ablility to "do it alone" as they say. One false move (which is always likely in this world) and you're finished! End of story, you failed. But Nature has created this process in such a way that any unconscious mechanism in us that could potentially interfere with the completion of this process or "mess it up" (when we sincerely want it to succeed from deep within our heart of hearts) has absolutely no potential to interfere with a positive result. How is this possible? It is easily possible because all of those doubtful, sabotaging mechanisms are actually a product of the Absence itself and by the time you have read this far, with a sincere heart, there is absolutely no way that that Absence has any potential to "get involved" with the process of eliminating it, because just by listening, you have been effectively positioned to stop identifying with it. So, as a result, this phenomenon can carry on all it wants to and generate thoughts and feelings of doubt, anxiety, and disbelief, but it will not change the fact that you have made your decision and that that phenomenon is about to become "history" in your experience.

So, if you are ready, at this point, you may now proceed to the next chapter.

If you are not ready and want more time, then that is okay,

too. All that you have to do is take whatever time you need and when you are feeling fed up enough and truly sick and tired of having to live with the influence of this phenomenon in your life, then all that you have to do is pick up this book and continue to proceed forward. We caution you, however, not to be tricked by thoughts which are being generated by the Absence itself, trying to convince you that you are not *perfectly* ready, that maybe you could be "more" ready, and perhaps it would "work better" if you gave yourself a little more time. This is all a lot of nonsense and basically a ploy on the part of this phenomenon to hopefully stick around for a little bit longer. The bottom line is that when you want it, you're ready. It's that simple. When that moment comes for you, please don't hesitate. There is no reason to.

Chapter 13

The Process—The Final Elimination of the Source of Fear

You are now ready to experience the final elimination of the source of fear, for yourself. You have already been through the main part of the process which is to read all of the information in this book up until this point, where you now have a chance to do the actual process itself which will fully generate the final elimination of this phenomenon from inside of your experience.

The process is quite simple and you have actually already done the hard part which is to have read most of this book. The next part is easy. All that you must do is follow a few, simple instructions which will align your consciousness with Omnipresence and the powerful forces of Nature and Evolution, and allow those forces the synergistic opportunity to act upon your simple desire and create the final elimination of the source of fear for you, personally.

Here are the instructions:
Begin by finding a quiet place that you can sit down in comfortably, preferably on the floor. If for any reason you are unable to sit comfortably on the floor for any length of time, then please start with a chair. It is not a good idea to change physical locations once you have begun the process. The process will work just fine in a chair, although we recommend the floor because it is easier to feel centered and grounded there. But if you are physically uncomfortable on the floor, you will not feel centered or grounded there anyway, so better to start with a chair where you can feel relaxed. But please use a chair where

175

you can sit upright and one that is not conducive to you falling asleep or going unconscious.

The next thing to do is to make sure that you will be undisturbed and have no interruptions. Unplug your phones and ask family members or friends that you live with to leave you undisturbed until you are finished.

Now keep this book with you and mark your place so that you can find it again easily.

Before we begin, we'd like to ask that you sit quietly for a little while, close your eyes and breathe naturally. Begin by taking a nice deep breath. Inhale... and exhale... Ahh.... Now relax your *whole* body and feel how effortless it is to breathe. Notice how your breath just happens, all by itself, with little or no effort on your part. There is a life force within, that causes you to breathe. Let your breath happen naturally as you relax even more.

Enjoy this experience for as long as you wish, and then pick up this book again, and read on.

Now that you are relaxed, we are going to ask you to close your eyes again, relax and take another deep breath. Inhale... Exhale... Ahhh... Now let go and allow yourself to become aware of how wonderfully your body takes care of itself, as you just sit and breathe naturally. Let go to your incredible human body and allow it to do its amazing work of supporting your existence here on this planet. Take another deep breath.

Inhale... Exhale... Ahhhh...

Now do that, and then pick up this book again and read on. (We are going to continue spending a little bit of time simply enjoying the experience of what it's like to just *be*.)

Now get ready to close your eyes again. Take another deep breath. Inhale... Exhale... Ahhh... Relax... Let yourself surrender to your body and your wonderful breath, let go, and now *feel the planet* beneath you. Feel the awesome presence of this beautiful planet earth. Become aware that you are seated on an awesomely powerful, blue/green jewel, residing in infinite space. There is nothing above you, below you, or on all sides of this amazing earth—just stars and infinite space; and the powerful presence of this awesome Universe! You are literally seated in space! You don't need a space ship, for this precious earth provides you with a most wonderful place from which to view the entire Universe. It is beautiful and provides you with the perfect environment from which to contemplate and experience your wonderful place in the Universe. Feel your lovely presence residing with great joy upon this wonderful sphere in the majestic beauty of your interplanetary kingdom of stars and the infinite Universe. Take some time now to enjoy the physical experience of sailing powerfully and perfectly through infinite space upon this giant and most precious blue jewel. Breathe deeply and relax even more.

When you are finished, pick up this book again and continue reading.

Now we are ready to begin. We are going to ask that you read the following statements, out loud, to yourself. Sit quietly and comfortably, take a deep breath and relax.

Now repeat the following slowly, and to yourself.

**I am love. I am power. I am Light.
I am Omnipresence.**

**I take full command of this emotional
spectrum of feeling, in light, in love, and in
the full presence of who I really am.
I take full command of this mental factor of**

intelligence in light, in love, and in the full presence of who I really am.

I take full command of this entire physical embodiment in light, in love, and in the full presence of who I really am.

I am Omnipresence.
So be it.

Now, take another deep breath. At this point, we are going to sit quietly for a little while and do nothing. This is the point at which the final elimination of the source of fear, can be fully effected within you.

There is nothing more for you to do. It is all in the hands of Omnipresence and the Universe, and the powerful forces of Nature and Evolution.

Sit quietly and relax. Close your eyes and just be. We will now take the time for this process to occur.

— —

— —

When you feel that the process is complete, take another deep breath. Do not expect to notice any big sensation. The final elimination of the source of fear is quiet and invisible, because it happens on another level of things.

Now, continue to sit quietly. Keep your eyes closed for a little while longer, relax, and feel your breath. As you breathe, you might begin to notice some lovely melodies or chimes. Feel yourself surrounded in the presence of angels. There is a clearness, a pristine quality of infinite space unbounded by anything artificial. Feel your heart soar in the clarity of this experience. Sit for a little while longer.

And now, you might notice a gentle wind of infinity. A primordial source of energy and presence that can move you to the core of your infinite self. This wind and the presence that it carries moves through your entire system in a magnificent cleansing of any remains of energy that are inappropriate and unconscious. Your entire system is being aligned with infinity and who you really are.

Now take another deep breath. Sit quietly and enjoy the experience of existing in space with the planets, the stars, and all of their majestic beauty and awesome, interstellar silence which speaks powerfully of their pure presence. Enjoy the deep, infinite nature of this primordial, unbounded existence in the stars. Your home is in the stars. That is where this beautiful earth resides. There never was any separation. It was all an illusion!

Now take your time and whenever you are ready, go ahead and open your eyes. Stretch your body gently, relax, and look around you. Breathe normally.

At this point, you may want to get up and go outdoors. See the sky, feel the air. Breathe in the intoxicating essence of Nature itself. Feel the earth beneath your feet.

At this point, you might think it would be fine to just go right back into your everyday routine and bombard yourself with phone calls, conversations, television, traffic, noise, or what-have-you. Try to wait before you do this. If at all possible, give yourself some space to just be with yourself for a little while and allow the results of the process to fully integrate within your system.

The final elimination of the source of fear can be a deceiving thing on the surface, because at first glace it sometimes looks as though nothing has happened! But if you are sensitive enough, you will recognize that indeed something very powerful has just occurred. Although you will not be able to measure it or "prove" it, you most definitely will begin to see the results during the process of your life unfolding.

The main thing to remember is that once this phenomenon has been eliminated, it *will not* come back. It is gone. Disappeared. Ceases to exists. There is no possible way that any person can ever get it to return, because our forward-moving evolution is too powerful. There is no way to go against the forces of evolution, and fortunately evolution never goes backwards.

And all that you need to do at this point is to simply relax and just be with yourself. You might notice a desire to feel, touch, and experience the simple things around you and notice that somehow your experience feels renewed. You may even notice a freshness, a newness, and most of all, a powerful sense of freedom coming from within. Or you may not notice any of these things and find yourself simply saying, "Gee, I'm not sure *what* just happened here." But that's all right, too. Everyone's experience is different and unique unto themselves. Some people will experience something powerful right away and others will not fully grasp what has happened until they see the results begin to unfold in their life.

And now here is another important point. Once you have completed this process, it is not necessary to ever go back and do it again. The results are permanent and complete. You may save the book and read it again for the purpose of understanding reverse-flow patterns. But you do not ever again have to go through the process of the final elimination of the source of fear. The most useful and most enlightening thing to do from this point on, is to point yourself forward and relish in the experience of a newfound, powerfully energized life, which can be imbued with your *presence*, finally, and afford you the miraculous opportunity of going forward and manifesting who you really are on this beautiful, planet earth.

Chapter 14

What Now?

Hopefully you have now allowed yourself plenty of space to be alone with your experience and assimilate the experience of the final elimination of the source of fear before turning to this chapter. If not, and you still feel that you could use some more time to just "be" and relax for a bit, then please take that time. There is really no hurry from this point on.

Once you are satisfied that you have taken sufficient time for yourself and are ready to go forward, then by all means pick up this chapter and we will tell you exactly how to do just that.

The single most important thing that is accomplished by the final elimination of the source of fear is that it gives you the opportunity to exist in full command of yourself and your life. When the source of fear is present, it is as though that phenomenon keeps you gripped in its energy and causes the main focus of your existence to exist in its own reverse-flow matrix of design, rather than in your own radiating flow of truth and Omnipresence. You will never feel as though your life is totally your own, because the fear generated by the existence of this thing will usually become the central, motivating factor of your existence, rather than love which is who you are. So what happens when the source of fear is eliminated? Let's look at a couple of diagrams to find out.

In the first drawing, Diagram A, on the next page, we see the source of fear well in place, causing a reverse-flow of energy and an accumulation of reverse-flow energy, patterns, and experiences. This person would find themselves gripped in

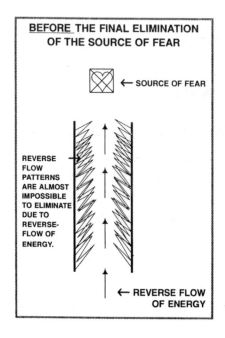

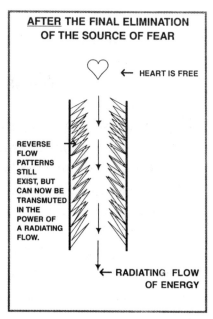

Diagram A

Diagram B

their patterns, acting them out, and finding it difficult or impossible to change them. The best they could hope for would be to somehow work around them or overcome them in some way, but this would take tremendous dedication and a massive effort on their part. Most people don't have that level of energy, having spent a life time co-existing with the source of fear. They are so tired, depleted, and in survival from the everyday struggle of living with this phenomenon, that they are just plain worn out.

In the second drawing, Diagram B, we see where the source of fear has been eliminated. The heart is now free and this person's presence is placed back in command of their reality. The heart can now freely emanate its bountiful, radiating flow of love. *But!* The patterns are still there, aren't they? As we

said earlier, the final elimination of the source of fear permanently eliminates the source of the problem, but now it is up to
you to do something about the patterns.

The incredible miracle that takes place after the source of
fear is eliminated, is that you will have unlimited power available to you to transmute the patterns *if* you take advantage of
that fact and make the effort.

One of the reasons that people are sometimes confused after
they complete this process is that they imagine that all of their
negative patterns are going to disappear as well. If they have a
fear-based pattern of, for example, feeling anxious every time
they meet someone new, and then that same pattern occurs
again after they have experienced the final elimination of the
source of fear, they might be surprised to find that they are
still feeling anxious and therefore think that the process didn't
work. "So what is the difference?" you might ask. The difference is actually quite profound. Before eliminating the source
of fear, that person would feel completely "gripped" in their
anxiety and unable to do anything to change it. The best they
could do would be to find ways of coping with it such as cov-
ering up the anxiety and trying to appear calm on the surface,
or avoiding the situation of meeting new people altogether.
Either way, the pattern runs the show because the Absence is
magnetically holding it there, no matter what. That person is
gripped by the source of fear and unable to exist in full command of their situation.

After the final elimination of the source of fear, all of this
changes. The pattern is still there, yes. But now this person has
a real choice as to whether it will continue to be there or not.
They can either continue to let the pattern run the show and
keep experiencing the anxiety *or* they can make a statement to
themselves that they are no longer willing to tolerate it. They

can then go into those anxiety-provoking situations from a place of love, purpose, and intent, *knowing that they are not the pattern*, and make every effort to interact with those new people from a real place of love and truth. The statement of intolerance for the pattern and the effort to interact with the people from a place of love and truth, positions that person's powerful presence in command of themselves and allows the energy of that presence to *flow through the pattern*, because there is no source of fear to stop it. This miraculously starts to *transmute* the pattern, which literally means to make it disappear! If this person really puts their energy into this only a few times, depending on the strength of the pattern, it is very likely that that pattern could be gone forever, never to return. An amazing thing happens when patterns are transmuted. Sometimes you can't even remember that they existed at all!

So after experiencing the final elimination of the source of fear, you can do one of two things. You can either sit back in your easy chair and do nothing, in which case you will still probably experience some powerful, positive change in your life, although it may take much longer to occur and may not be as dramatic (but then again, it might!) or you can take a very active position in your life and put your energy into making the positive changes that you want to see happen for yourself, in which case, *anything* is possible!

The best way to approach your life after you have experienced the final elimination of the source of fear is to focus on a vision of something that you want, that is or always has been your heart's desire. Take advantage of your newfound strength and *test it out*. Realize that you now have the ability to achieve whatever you want in your life, if you are willing to make the effort. The final elimination of the source of fear is the single, most empowering thing that a person can do for themselves because it is the one thing that can place that individual in a position of full command over themselves, in a way that is unimpeded and allows them the greatest possible power in whatever they do in love.

Let the light shine through, enjoy life, and take full advantage of your infinitely empowered situation, in love, light, truth, and in the fullest presence of who you really are. Enjoy!

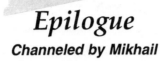

Epilogue
Channeled by Mikhail

My dearest, most beloved friend. In that you have taken the time and the most precious energy of your lifeforce to complete this illuminating process, then indeed, you are blessed. You are a rose among the stars and all of the heavens await the magical unfoldment of your most beautiful, beloved presence.

Do you know how loved you are? How important you are? Do you know how much it means to all who love this earth that you have held the courage and the fortitude within yourself to hold fast to the truth, take a stand in Love, and empower yourself with the infinite raiment of your divine, immortal presence?

Indeed, it is true, that in most ways you have forgotten yourself on this magnificently beautiful, pristine sphere of life that you so belovingly call your precious, planetary earth.

But nonetheless, your heart has risen to the stars and you have taken your divine place among those of us who care deeply for this entire Universe and all of the precious life that it holds.

Dear friend, it is only a matter of time before your precious, physical body attunes to the magic of your divine, immortal presence. You need not believe any longer that you must force anything, for in surrender lies the key to eternal bliss. You are a breath of life, a flower in the heavens, a majestic and powerful god among the Universes and in that acknowledgment I behold, in you, a presence unlike any other for you are, indeed, the divine manifestation of Omnipresence itself.

Come join us in the stars. Allow the great brilliance of your consciousness to unfold itself in a divine meeting of the gods, those who produce life and powerful evolution among the gracious planetary spheres of life. Although you exist upon the earth, you are here with us as well, for all things in creation exist as one great, bright unfoldment of Love and the absolute purity of that emotion.

Be not in a state of despair for all that has occurred upon your beloved planet in its more recent history of several millenniums past, for you have contributed deeply into this mysterious blue jewel called earth and have, in your own individual effort, moved and uplifted the entire, collective consciousness to a new, more empowered state of being.

Be not a stranger to your precious earth and to all of its wondrous creatures. Offer them your love for indeed they are all in desperate need of human support and companionship. Love the earth as you love yourself, for you and this beautiful planet are one and the same. A divine expression of one another.

Pay no attention to those who ridicule and make light of your current, collective state of suffering for they are not speaking the truth and their hearts are dying from within.

But behold! A majestic light emerges from the powerful, infinity of Love itself and shall resurrect all who live in the chains and suffering of this enormous beast. It is a certainty, so therefore rejoice within your heart of hearts for help is coming and help, has indeed, arrived.

I love you.
Mikhail

FOR MORE INFORMATION

For information on Telstar events, workshops, and lectures with Saratoga, plus announcements of new audio tapes and future publications, you may request to be placed on Telstar's mailing list by sending your name and address to:

TELSTAR
PO BOX 59832
Potomac, MD 20859 USA
301-294-5954
www.telstarnova.com

TO ORDER ADDITIONAL BOOKS

You may order additional copies of *The Final Elimination of the Source of Fear* by writing to the publisher at the following address:

TELSTAR
PO BOX 59832
Potomac, MD 20859 USA
301-294-5954
www.telstarnova.com

Include a check (U.S. residents only) or money order for $11.95 USD per copy, plus shipping as follows: For U.S. orders, add $4.00 for the first book plus $1.25 for each additional book. For Canadian residents, add $6.00 USD for the first book, plus $1.50 USD for each additional book. New Mexico residents add 5.5625% sales tax to the total amount.

Make funds payable to *Nova Publications*. All payments must be in *US dollars*.

For shipment to countries other than the U.S. and Canada, please contact the publisher for shipping rates.

Quantity discounts are also available. Information will be provided upon request.